EYEWITNESS TRAVEL

TOP 10

MIAMI
& THE KEYS

WITHDRAWN

JEFFREY KENNEDY

P9-CNH-650

DK | Penguin Random House

Top 10 Miami and the Keys Highlights

The Top 10 of Everything

CONTENTS

Miami and the Keys Area by Area

Streetsmart

Within each Top 10 list in this book, no hierarchy of quality or popularity is implied. All 10 are, in the editor's opinion, of roughly equal merit.
    Throughout this book, floors are referred to in accordance with American usage; i.e., the "first floor" is at ground level.

Front cover and spine *Art Deco Avalon Hotel on South Beach's Ocean Drive*
Back cover *Lush green islands of the Keys archipelago*
Title page *Brightly colored lifeguard station on South Beach*

Welcome to
Miami and the Keys

Miami is a glamorous tropical city, where wide sandy beaches and palm trees give way to Art Deco hotels, throbbing nightlife, cutting-edge contemporary art, and a vibrant Latino culture. To the south, the Keys are a string of reef-fringed islands, sprinkled with white-sand beaches and culminating at party-loving Key West. With Eyewitness Top 10 Miami and the Keys, it is yours to explore.

Miami's hedonistic heart is **South Beach**: elegant and stylish, with fine dining and fashionable shopping. Everything ultimately revolves around the beach itself, an enticing stretch of sand backed by hip hotels. The skyscrapers of **Downtown** Miami, by contrast, harbor historic sights and intriguing museums, while nearby **Little Havana** is the hub of everything Cuban, from traditional fruit-juice stalls to cigar factories. North of Downtown lie the **Wynwood murals** and the trendy stores of the **Design District**, and **Little Haiti** is one of the city's most exuberant ethnic enclaves.

Meanwhile, at Florida's southern tip, the **Keys** are an archipelago of over 10,000 tiny islands of which fewer than 50 are inhabited. Just offshore lies the Florida Reef, a great wall of living coral with a dazzling array of marine life. **Key West** boasts museums and **The Hemingway Home**, lively bars, and spectacular sunsets.

Whether you're coming for a weekend or a week, our Top 10 guide brings together the best of everything Miami and the Keys can offer, from hip South Beach to authentic Cuban diners. The guide has useful tips throughout, from seeking out what's free to avoiding the crowds, plus nine easy-to-follow itineraries, designed to tie together a clutch of sights in a short space of time. Add inspiring photography and detailed maps, and you've got the essential pocket-sized travel companion. **Enjoy the book, and enjoy Miami and the Keys.**

Clockwise from top: **Bahia Honda State Park, Atlantic coral reef at Key Largo, Ocean Drive, Miami skyline, Art Deco fountain, tearoom at Vizcaya museum, Sloppy Joe's bar at Key West**

Exploring Miami and the Keys

There are so many things to do in Miami and the Keys, you could easily spend a couple of weeks here. Whether you're visiting for a weekend or have the luxury of an extra couple of days, these two- and four-day itineraries will help you make the most of your time.

The Biscayne Bay boat tour is a very popular way of seeing the sights.

The Wolfsonian–FIU boasts an extensive assemblage of modern design.

Two Days in Miami

Day ❶
MORNING
Begin by having breakfast at **Bayside Marketplace** (see p92), followed by a boat tour of Biscayne Bay (see p59). Afterwards stroll to Downtown Miami, taking in the exhibits and gardens at the **Pérez Art Museum** (see p91).
AFTERNOON
Head to **South Beach** (see pp12–13) for lunch on the seafront, before soaking up the Art Deco heritage along **Collins and Washington avenues** (see p13). Be sure to make time for the **Wolfsonian–FIU** (see pp28–9) and **Lincoln Road Mall** (see p82), before getting back to the beach for dinner and to soak up the **South Beach nightlife** (see p87).

Day ❷
MORNING
Start the day in **Little Havana** (see pp18–19) for a traditional Cuban breakfast at **Versailles** (see p97). Visit the **Little Havana Cigar Factory** (see p19) and the **Calle Ocho Walk of Fame** (see p19) before touring the **Vizcaya Museum and Gardens** (see pp20–21).

Mahogany Hammock Trail

Everglades National Park

Key
— Two-day itinerary
— Four-day itinerary

Key West

Bahia Honda State Park

AFTERNOON
Take a tour of **Coral Gables** (see pp24–5), before checking out the work at the **Lowe Art Museum** (see pp26–7). End the day with dinner at the **Biltmore Hotel** (see p24).

Four Days in Miami and the Keys

Day ❶
MORNING
Sample **South Beach** (see pp12–13) life with breakfast at **News Café** (see p88), then wander along Collins and Washington avenues to admire the **Art Deco District** (see pp14–17), stopping at the **Wolfsonian–FIU** (see pp28–9).

Miami

See inset map, above

Head to Coral Gables for lunch at **the Biltmore** *(see p24)*.

AFTERNOON

After lunch take in some of George Merrick's fabulous architecture around **Coral Gables** *(see pp24–5)*, and the exhibits at the **Lowe Art Museum** *(see pp26–7)*. End the day at the **Vizcaya Museum and Gardens** *(see pp20–21)*.

Day ❷

MORNING

Spend the day exploring the **Gold Coast via Highway A1A** *(see pp30–31)*, beginning with breakfast on the **Broadwalk** *(see p31)*. Explore **John U. Lloyd Beach State Park** *(see p30)* before taking lunch on **Las Olas Boulevard** *(see p30)*, Fort Lauderdale.

AFTERNOON

Head up the coast to Palm Beach, touring the **Flagler Museum** *(see p30)*, **The Breakers** hotel *(see p30)*, and the opulent **Worth Avenue** *(see p30)* before heading back to Miami.

Day ❸

MORNING

Stroll around **Downtown Miami** *(see pp90–7)*, then either **take a boat tour of Biscayne Bay**, or peruse exhibits at the **Pérez Art Museum** *(see p91)*. Head to **Little Havana** *(see pp18–19)* for lunch at **Versailles** *(see p97)*.

AFTERNOON

Head out to the **Everglades National Park** *(see pp34–5)* for the afternoon, getting a taster at **Shark Valley**, **Mahogany Hammock**, and the **Anhinga and Gumbo Limbo trails**.

Day ❹

MORNING

Get up early to drive Hwy-1 to **Key West** *(see pp32–3)*, stopping for a dip along the way at **Bahia Honda State Park** *(see p121)*, and maybe a picnic.

AFTERNOON

Visit the **Hemingway Home** *(see p32)* and the **Mel Fisher Maritime Museum** *(see p122)* in Key West. Watch the sun set over **Mallory Square** *(see p32)*, and end the day with a "Duval Crawl" down **Duval Street** *(see p32)*.

Bahia Honda State Park has one of the best beaches in the world.

Top 10 Miami and the Keys Highlights

Art Deco apartments on Miami Beach

TOP 10 Miami and the Keys Highlights

Miami is all pastel hues and warm, velvety zephyrs – a tropical reverie. The culture is sensuous, often spiked with Caribbean accents. Outdoor activities hold sway throughout the area, at the beaches and in the turquoise waters; the vibrant nightlife attracts pleasure-seekers; and historical sights abound.

1 South Beach

Ever since *Miami Vice (see p83)* drew attention to this fun-zone, hedonists have flocked here for the beaches and nightlife *(see pp12–13)*.

2 Art Deco District

The whimsical architecture on South Beach traces its roots back to 1920s Paris *(see p17)*, but underwent an exotic transformation and blossomed into Florida's own Tropical Deco *(see pp14–15)*.

3 Calle Ocho, Little Havana

This street is still the heart of Cuban Miami, with local coffee shops, cafes, and markets selling *cafecitos*, *batidos* and tropical fruits *(see pp18–19)*.

4 Vizcaya Museum and Gardens

One immensely rich man's aspiration to European grandeur and appreciation of Western artistic heritage led to the creation of Miami's most beautiful cultural treasure *(see pp20–21)*.

5 Merrick's Coral Gables Fantasies

The 1920s boom saw a need to build not only structures but also an identity. George Merrick rose to the challenge and created fantasy wonderlands that continue to stir the imagination today *(see pp24–5)*.

CAROL CITY
826
924
WESTVIEW
HIALEAH
GLADEVIEW
MIAMI SPRINGS
BROWNSVILLE
826
836
WEST MIAMI
Calle Ocho, Little Havana **3**
Merrick's Coral Gables Fantasies **5**
CORAL WAY VILLAGE
CORAL GABLES **4**
6
874
Lowe Art Museum
Vizcaya Museum and Gardens
SOUTH MIAMI
KENDALL
PINECREST

0 km 5
0 miles 5

South Florida

The Everglades

Gulf of Mexico

The Keys

Atlantic Ocean

Key West

0 km   50
0 miles   50

GOLDEN GLADES

NORTH MIAMI

SURFSIDE

MIAMI SHORES

MIAMI BEACH

① South Beach

② Art Deco District

⑦ SoBe

The Wolfsonian–FIU

DOWNTOWN MIAMI

⑧ Gold Coast Highway A1A

Key Biscayne

⑥ Lowe Art Museum

This significant art museum showcases around 17,500 works of art, including masterpieces from cultures the world over, and from every age (see pp26–7).

The Wolfsonian–FIU ⑦

This superb museum (which began life as a storage company) owes much to its founder's passion for collecting 20th-century propaganda art and design artifacts of the period 1885–1945 (see pp28–9).

⑧ Gold Coast Highway A1A

Hugging the sands of the beautiful Gold Coast, Highway A1A wends its way through Florida's wealthiest and most beautiful areas (see pp30–31).

Key West ⑨

This mythic area lives up to its reputation as the most outlandishly free spot in the US. A frothy mix of maritime traditions and laid-back style (see pp32–3).

⑩ The Everglades

Taking up most of South Florida, the Everglades is a vast sea of swamp and sawgrass, dotted with subtropical forests and populated with prolific wildlife. It is also home to Native American Seminoles and Miccosukees (see pp34–5).

TOP 10 ⭐ South Beach

SoBe, the nickname for Miami's beautiful South Beach, was inspired by Manhattan's SoHo, and it's become every bit as hip and fashionable as its New York counterpart. Now the "American Riviera" offers an ebullient mix of beach life, club-crawling, lounge-lizarding, and alternative chic, attracting devotees from around the globe. Yet, SoBe's chic modern character is also nicely blended with just the right amount of light-hearted kitsch.

① Lincoln Road Mall

Built in the 1920s as an upscale shopping district, the Lincoln Road Mall **(below)** became a pedestrian mall in the 1960s. This fashionable area is lined with restaurants, shops, and galleries.

③ Lifeguard Huts

After a hurricane in 1992 destroyed most of the lifeguard stations, several artists were called in to create fun replacements. The best of these stands can be found between 10th and 16th streets **(right)**.

② The Villa by Barton G.

This Mediterranean Revival style building houses a hotel and a restaurant run by renowned restaurateur Barton G. Weiss. Gianni Versace once lived in the mansion.

④ News Café

The café-restaurant continues to be action central for SoBe social life. Sit and read one of the morning papers over a full breakfast – or just watch the action unfold on Ocean Drive *(see p88)*.

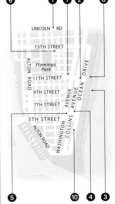

NEED TO KNOW

MAP S6

The Villa by Barton G.: restaurant open from 7pm daily; www.villa bartong.com

Miami Beach Cinematheque: www. mbcinema.com

■ Parking is a problem in the area, so once you find a place, leave the car and walk. You'll need to feed the meter a feast of coins (many meters now accept bills and credit cards), unless you choose one of the parking garages.

■ To participate fully in the SoBe experience, the News Café *(see p88)* should definitely be your destination for people-watching.

Map of South Beach

7 Old City Hall

The buff-colored 1920s Mediterranean Revival tower **(left)** is a distinctive SoBe landmark. Its red-tile roof can be seen for blocks around. The building now houses the Miami Beach Cinematheque movie theater.

LGBT+ RENAISSANCE

South Beach is a top destination for LGBT+ travelers. Rainbow flags dotted throughout indicate gay-friendly businesses. The festivals, all-night events, and beach parties attract thousands from around the world. Many hotels offer packages geared toward LGBT+ guests. A Body Beautiful culture thrives here, and, along with the constant ebb and flow of revelers, makes the area a great place to meet like-minded people.

9 SoBe Clubs

Most of South Beach's top clubs are located on Washington and Collins avenues, between 5th and 24th streets. Few get going until at least midnight. There are a wide variety of venues to choose from (see pp86–7).

10 Ocean Drive

Strolling, skating, or biking along this beachfront strip is the way the locals do it. Take in the toned, tanned athletes, the abundant, ice-cream-colored Art Deco architecture (see pp14–17), and the people-watching cafés.

5 Collins and Washington Avenues

These funkier cousins of Ocean Drive offer kinky shops and fine Art Deco buildings, including the Miami Beach Post Office.

8 Lummus Park Beach

This swath of busy park and 300-ft (90-m) wide beach **(below)** stretches for ten blocks from 5th St north. Much of the lovely sand was imported.

6 Española Way

This Mediterranean Revival enclave is all salmon-colored stucco, stripy awnings, and red-tile roofs. Built in 1922–5, it was meant to be an artists' colony but instead became a red-light district at one stage. It now houses boutiques and offbeat art galleries.

🔟 ⭐ Art Deco District

The Art Deco District of South Beach consists of approximately 800 beautifully preserved buildings, the cream of them along Ocean Drive. This splendid array of structures embodies Miami's unique interpretation of the Art Deco style, which took the world by storm in the 1920s and 1930s. Florida's take on it is often called Tropical Deco, which befits the fun-and-sun approach to life. Often hotels were designed to look like ocean liners (Nautical Moderne) or styled with curving, streamlined features (Streamline Moderne).

Colony Hotel ①
Perhaps the most famous of the Deco hotels along here, primarily because its blue neon sign **(right)**, has featured in so many movies and TV series.

② Beacon Hotel
The abstract decoration above the ground floor of the hotel has been brightened by a contemporary color scheme, an example of "Deco Dazzle," introduced by designer Leonard Horowitz in the 1980s.

③ Breakwater Hotel
The Streamline Moderne hotel **(below)** was built in 1939. It features blue and white racing stripes and a striking central tower that recalls both a ship's funnel and Native American totems.

④ Park Central
A 1937 favorite by Henry Hohauser, the most famous architect in Miami at the time. Here he used the nautical theme to great effect.

⑤ Waldorf Towers
Here stands one of the first examples (1937) of Nautical Moderne, where the style is carried to one of its logical extremes with the famous ornamental lighthouse on the hotel's roof. Fantasy towers were the stock-in-trade for Deco architects.

⑥ Cardozo Hotel
A late Hohauser work (1939) and the favorite of Barbara Baer Capitman (see p17), this is a Streamline masterpiece, in which the detail of traditional Art Deco is replaced with beautifully rounded sides, aerodynamic racing stripes, and other expressions of the modern age. The terrazzo floor utilizes this cheap version of marble to stylish effect. The hotel was reopened in 1982 and is now owned by the Cuban-American singer Gloria Estefan.

7 Cavalier Hotel

A traditional Art Deco hotel **(left)**, which provides a contrast to the later Cardozo next door. Where the Cardozo emphasizes the horizontal and vaguely nautical, this facade is starkly vertical and temple-like. The temple theme is enhanced by beautifully ornate vertical stucco friezes, which recall the abstract, serpentine geometric designs of the Aztecs and other Meso-American cultures.

8 The Tides

An Art Deco masterpiece, the Tides resembles a luxury ocean liner. All 45 spacious suites have expansive ocean views, and each guest is assigned a dedicated personal assistant. The Goldeneye Suite has a hot tub at the center of the room.

9 Essex House

Hohauser's Essex House **(below)** is considered one of the best examples of maritime Art Deco architecture. Erected in 1938, the stark, white building closely resembles a ship, with "porthole" windows and awnings that look like railings. It isn't difficult to find this landmark; just look for the neon-lit spire.

Map of the Art Deco District

NEED TO KNOW
MAP S4

Art Deco Welcome Center: 1001 Ocean Drive at 10th; 305-672-2014; open 10am–5pm daily (to 7pm Thu), museum closed Mon; adm $5; guided walking tours 10:30am daily (also 6:30pm Thu), other guided tours and self-guided audio tours are available at the center; adm (for tours) $25, concessions $20; www.art decowelcomecenter.com

■ Mango's Tropical Café *(see p88)* is florid and steamy, and always very happening.

10 Leslie Hotel

The Leslie (1937) is white and yellow with gray accents **(above)** – a color scheme much in favor along Ocean Drive. Originally, however, Deco coloring was quite plain, usually white with only the trim in colors. Inside are shades of turquoise and flamingo pink.

Tropical Deco Features

Neon lights creating a blaze of color after sundown on Ocean Drive

1 Neon

Used mostly for outlining architectural elements, neon lighting, in a range of colors, came into its own with Tropical Deco.

2 Ice-Cream Colors

Most Deco buildings here were originally white, with a bit of painted trim; the present-day rich pastel palette "Deco Dazzle" was the innovation of Miami designer and Capitman collaborator Leonard Horowitz in the 1980s.

3 Nautical Features

There's no better way to remind visitors of the ocean and its pleasures than with portholes and ship railings. Some of the buildings resemble beached liners.

4 Curves and Lines

This suggestion of speed is the core of the Streamline Moderne style – it is an implicit appreciation of the power of technology.

5 Tropical Motifs

These motifs include Florida palms, panthers, orchids, and alligators, but especially birds, such as flamingos and cranes.

6 Stylized, Geometric Patterning

This was a nod to the extreme modernity of Cubism, as well as the power and precision of technology, espoused by Bauhaus precepts.

7 Stucco Bas-Relief Friezes

These sculptural bands provided Art Deco designers with endless possibilities for a wonderful mix of ancient and modern motifs and themes for the buildings.

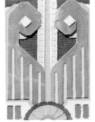

Stucco frieze, Cavalier Hotel

8 Fantasy Towers

Many Art Deco buildings try to give the viewer a sense of some-thing mythical – towers that speak of far shores or exalted visions – and that effectively announce the hotel's name, as well.

9 Chrome

Nothing says "modern" quite like a cool and incorruptible silver streak of chrome. This material is used as detailing on and within many Deco buildings.

10 Glass Blocks

Used in the construction of many Deco walls, the glass blocks give a sense of lightness in a part of the country where indoor-outdoor living is a year-round lifestyle.

THE STORY OF TROPICAL DECO

The Art Deco style took the world stage following the 1925 Exposition in Paris, synthesizing all sorts of influences, from Art Nouveau's flowery forms and Bauhaus to Egyptian imagery and the geometric patterns of Cubism. In 1930s America, Art Deco buildings reflected the belief that technology was the way forward, absorbing the speed and edginess of the Machine Age as well as the fantasies of science fiction and even a tinge of ancient mysticism. The thrilling new style was just what was needed to counteract the gloom of the Great Depression and give Americans a coherent vision for the future. In Miami, the style was exuberantly embraced and embellished upon with the addition of numerous local motifs, becoming "Tropical Deco." Its initial glory days were not to last long, however. Many hotels became soldiers' barracks in World War II and were torn down afterward. Fortunately, Barbara Baer Capitman *(see p39)* fought a famous battle to preserve these buildings. The Miami Beach Historic District was designated in 1979.

TOP 10 ARCHITECTS

1 Henry Hohauser: Park Central, Colony, Edison, Cardozo, Governor, Essex, Webster, Century, Taft

2 Albert Anis: Clevelander, Waldorf, Avalon, Majestic, Abbey, Berkeley Shore, Olympic

3 Anton Skislewicz: Breakwater, Kenmore

4 L. Murray Dixon: Tiffany, Palmer House, Fairmont, Tudor, Senator, St. Moritz

5 Igor B. Polevitsky: Shelborne

6 Roy F. France: Cavalier

7 Robert Swartburg: Delano, The Marseilles

8 Kichnell & Elliot: Carlyle

9 Henry O. Nelson: Beacon

10 Russell Pancoast: Bass Museum

Example of Streamline Moderne style

The bright pastel colors of the "Deco Dazzle" style, the creation of Leonard Horowitz, is perfectly portrayed in the Hotel Avalon building.

🔟 ⭐ Calle Ocho, Little Havana

Little Havana has been the heart of the Cuban community since they first started fleeing Cuba in the 1960s. Don't expect much in the way of sights – your time here is best spent soaking up the atmosphere in the streets. The area's heart is Southwest 8th Street, better known by its Spanish name, Calle Ocho. Its liveliest stretch, between SW 11th and SW 17th avenues, can be enjoyed on foot, but other points of interest are more easily reached by car.

1 **Plaza de la Cubanidad**
At the plaza is a bronze map of Cuba (**above**) and an enigmatic quote by Cuban revolutionary hero José Martí.

2 **Brigade 2506 Memorial on Cuban Memorial Boulevard**
An eternal flame honors the Cuban-Americans who died in the Bay of Pigs invasion of Cuba in 1961. Other memorials pay tribute to Cuban heroes Antonio Maceo and José Martí, who fought against Spanish colonialism in the 1800s.

3 **Dominos Park**
For decades, male Cubans have gathered at the corner of SW 15th Ave to match wits over games of dominoes (**above**). The pavilion and patio were built in 1976.

4 **Little Havana To Go**
If you're looking for Cuban memorabilia, this is the store for you. You'll find cigars and art, and there's even a replica of a 1958 telephone book (see p96).

NEED TO KNOW

MAP K3

Botánica El Aguila Vidente: 1122 SW 8th St; 305-854-4086

Little Havana Cigar Factory: 1501 SW 8th St; 305-541-1103; open 10am–6pm daily

■ You will have an easier time in this district if you can speak a good bit of Spanish, especially in shops or when phoning establishments.

■ Make sure you try the Cuban sampler platter at Versailles, with sweet plantains, cassava, and a Cuban tamale.

6 Calle Ocho Walk of Fame

Imitating Hollywood, pink marble stars embedded in the sidewalks (left) recognize not only Cuban celebrities, beginning with salsa singer Celia Cruz in 1987, but also all famous Hispanics with any ties to South Florida.

TOP 10 CUBAN CULTURAL IMPORTS

1 Cigars
2 Salsa, mambo, bolero, merengue (rhythms)
3 Santería (mystical belief system)
4 Spanish language
5 Cafecito (Cuban coffee)
6 Black beans and plantains
7 Guayabera shirts
8 Gloria Estefan
9 The Buena Vista Social Club (movie)
10 Before Night Falls (movie)

10 Botánica El Aguila Vidente

This botánica (traditional folk medicine shop) is one of several establishments offering paraphernalia and spiritual consultations, practices used in the Caribbean religion of Santería (see p56).

Map of Calle Ocho, Little Havana

La Carreta restaurant in the heart of Little Havana

5 José Martí Riverfront Park

This small, pretty park was dedicated in 1985 to the Cuban struggle for freedom. The site became a Tent City for many of the homeless Mariel boatlift refugees in 1980.

7 Versailles

A trip to Miami is not complete without at least a snack at this legendary institution. Versailles is a Cuban version of a fancy diner, with mirrors everywhere and a constant hubbub (see p97).

8 Woodlawn Cemetery

Here lie the remains of two former Cuban presidents, including Gerardo Machado, as well as Nicaraguan dictator Anastasio Somoza.

9 Little Havana Cigar Factory

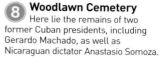

This is an inviting store and lounge (left) with stylish wooden and leather decor inspired by 1950s cigar clubs.

TOP 10 ⭐ Vizcaya Museum and Gardens

A trumped-up pastiche it may be, but the Vizcaya Museum is undeniably grand, with the feel of a European-inspired mansion, exactly what its makers – industrial magnate James Deering, designer Paul Chalfin, and architect F. Burrall Hoffman – intended when they built it in the early 1900s. Embodying a 400-year range of styles, both the genuine and ersatz have been skillfully assembled to evoke another culture, another continent, and another age.

1 Formal Gardens

The villa's elaborate gardens, extending over 10 acres (4 ha), will probably give you the greatest pleasure. The splashing fountains of gracefully carved stone, statuary **(above)**, and cleverly laid-out formal plantings offer myriad harmonious and ever-changing vistas. The evocative Secret Garden and playful Maze Garden conceal great artistry.

2 East Loggia

This portico frames magnificent views out over the sea and of the quaint stone breakwater known as the Barge. Carved in the shape of a large ship, it provides a perfect foreground to Key Biscayne, which lies just off the coast.

3 Italian Renaissance Dining Room

Another echo of the antique Italian taste, with a 2,000-year-old Roman table, a pair of 16th-century tapestries, and a full set of 17th-century chairs.

4 Italian Renaissance Living Room

The largest room in the house, the living room includes notable pieces, such as a 2,000-year-old marble Roman tripod, a tapestry depicting the *Labors of Hercules*, a 15th-century Hispano-Moresque rug, and a Neapolitan altar screen.

5 Neo-Classical Entrance Hall and Library

The mood, although still 18th-century, is much more sober in these rooms **(right)** in the English Neo-Classical style, inspired by the work of Robert Adam.

6 Empire Bathroom

Few bathrooms in the world are more ornate than this marble, silver, and gilded affair. The bathtub was designed by Deering to run either fresh- or saltwater from the Biscayne Bay.

DEERING'S DREAM

Money was no object for industrialist James Deering. He wanted his winter residence to provide a sense of family history as well as luxury. Thus he bought and shipped bits of European pomp and reassembled them on this ideal spot right by the sea.

7 Rococo Music Room

All flowers and fluff, the music room **(above)** is graced with an exquisite Italian harpsichord dating from 1619, a dulcimer, and a harp.

Floorplan of the Vizcaya Museum and Gardens

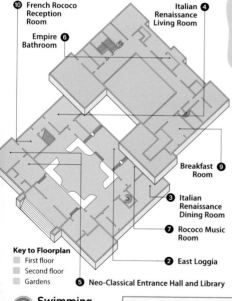

⑩ French Rococo Reception Room

Empire Bathroom ⑥

Italian Renaissance Living Room ④

Breakfast Room ⑨

③ Italian Renaissance Dining Room

⑦ Rococo Music Room

② East Loggia

⑤ Neo-Classical Entrance Hall and Library

Key to Floorplan
- First floor
- Second floor
- Gardens

9 Breakfast Room

On the upper floor, four ceramic Chinese Foo dogs guard the steps that ascend to what is probably the most bombastic room in the house.

10 French Rococo Reception Room

The assemblage is a mix of styles, but the overall look is of a salon under the 18th-century French King Louis XV. The tinted-plaster ceiling is from a Venetian palace.

8 Swimming Pool

This swimming pool extends under the house. Its walls are decorated with sea shells and depictions of marine life, and there are frescoes on the ceiling. The design is reminiscent of Italian homes on the canals of Venice.

NEED TO KNOW

MAP L6 ■ 3251 South Miami Ave ■ 305-250-9133 ■ www.vizcaya museum.org

Open 9:30am–4:30pm Wed–Mon (Thanksgiving and Christmas Day closed)

Adm $18; children $6; under-6s free

■ Take the guided tour for lots of juicy gossip about Mr. Deering's posh ways, as well as various legends, superstitions and quirks about many of the furnishings.

■ The café and shop have been closed for repairs after the damage caused by Hurricane Irma in 2017.

Following pages Vizcaya Museum and Gardens

TOP 10 ⭐ Merrick's Coral Gables Fantasies

Coral Gables is a separate city within Greater Miami. Aptly described as the City Beautiful, its swanky homes line avenues shaded by giant banyans and oak, backing up to canals. Regulations ensure that new buildings use the same architectural vocabulary advocated by George Merrick when he planned the community in the 1920s. Undeniably he created a wonderland of a place that has not lost its aesthetic impact.

Biltmore Hotel ①

George Merrick's 1926 masterpiece has been refurbished and burnished to its original splendor **(right)** and remains one of the most stunning hotels in the country. It served as a military hospital during World War II and was a veteran's hospital until 1968. The 315-ft (96-m) near-replica of Seville's Giralda Tower is a local landmark (see p148).

② French Normandy Village

The most homogeneous of all the villages at Coral Gables, this is all open timberwork, white stucco, and shake (cedar) roofs. Little alcoves and gardens here and there complete the picture-postcard look.

③ Venetian Pool

The boast that this is the most beautiful swimming pool in the world **(below)** is a fair one. Incorporating a cave and waterfalls, it was fashioned from a coral rock quarry in 1923 by Merrick's associates, Phineas Paist and Denman Fink (see p107).

Map of Merrick's Coral Gables

SEVILLA AV
ANASTASIA AV
LE JEUNE RD
BIRD RD
GRANADA BLVD
RIVIERA DRIVE
BLUE RD
CORAL GABLES
SW 57TH AV
UNIVERSITY
Lake Osceola ⑥
University 🚉
SOUTH DIXIE HIGHWAY
RIVIERA DRIVE
HARDEE RD
SOUTH MIAMI

4 French Country Village

Seven mansions are built in various styles typical of the French countryside. Some have open timber, stone, red brick, and shake (cedar) roofs, while others resemble the classic grange.

MERRICK THE VISIONARY

Merrick's dream was to build an American Venice. The project was the biggest real estate venture of the 1920s, costing around $100 million. The hurricane of 1926 then the Wall Street crash of 1929 left his city incomplete and Merrick himself destitute, but what remains is proof of his imagination.

5 Chinese Village

An entire block has been transformed into a walled Chinese enclave. The curved, glazed-tile roofs peek above the trees in vibrant colors, with Chinese red and yellow, and bamboo motifs predominating.

6 Dutch South African Village

This collection of homes (right) embodies the high-peaked facades and scrolls of typical Dutch architecture, along with white stucco walls and red roofs associated with the Mediterranean. The style evolved as Boers adapted to African climes.

7 French City Village

Here you'll find nine graceful *petits palais* in the grand French style, looking as if a city block of Paris has been airlifted to the US. The most elaborate confection is on the north corner of Cellini and Hardee.

NEED TO KNOW

MAP F3

Venetian Pool: 2701 De Soto Blvd; 305-460-5306; open times vary seasonally; closed national holidays

Congregational Church: 3010 De Soto Blvd; 305-448-7421; services 9am and 11am Sun

■ Driving in Coral Gables can be tricky. Many of the streets have two names, and the signs are spelled out on stucco blocks at ground level, which can be hard to read at night.

■ Sample the salads and soups at Books and Books (265 Aragon Ave).

8 Florida Pioneer Village

These are imitations of the early plantation and colonial homes built by Florida's first aristocrats. The style incorporates Neo-Classical, columned porches with the stucco walls of tropical tradition.

10 Italian Village

The typical country type of Italian villa, with its red-tile roof and painted stucco walls can be found here. Many later constructions have carried on the theme, so the original Merrick creations are almost lost in the mix.

9 Congregational Church

Coral Gables' first church (below), built by Merrick in Spanish Baroque style, is a replica of a church in Costa Rica.

TOP 10 ★ Lowe Art Museum

Miami's premier art venue, the Lowe was founded in 1950, and built in 1950–52 thanks to a donation from philanthropists Joe and Emily Lowe. More than 17,500 pieces showcase many of the world's most important artistic traditions, including those of the Renaissance and Baroque eras. Expansion to the galleries is now necessary to display the complete collection, but nevertheless, the most significant works are always on display, unless on loan to other museums.

7 Ancient American

The collection covers all eras and areas, from about 1500 BC to the 16th century. A silver disk from 14th-century Peru is a rare piece and the wood figurine from Columbia (**below**) is notable.

1 Contemporary Glass and Studio Arts

This stunning $3.5 million glass collection (**above**) features works by Dale Chihuly, Richard Jolley, and William Carlson.

4 Native American

A Seminole shoulder bag, beautifully embroidered using thousands of tiny, colored-glass trade beads, is the pride of this collection. Also on show are Najavo, Hopi, and Apache art forms, which include masks, textiles, pottery, basketry, and wooden *kachina* dolls.

2 Asian

One of the museum's strongest collections, with superb Chinese ceramics (**right**), as well as bronze and jade pieces, and other ceramics from Neolithic times to the 20th century. There is also classic, folk, and tribal art from India.

5 Latin American

Important holdings of 20th-century art by Hispanic artists include Fernando Botero of Colombia, Arnaldo Roche-Rabell of Puerto Rico, and Carlos Alfonzo, who was born in Cuba.

3 Egyptian

This excellent collection includes Coptic textiles, and there is also a jewel-like portrait sarcophagus mask, intended to resemble the features of the deceased.

6 17th-Century to Contemporary European and American

Some extraordinary works from this collection on permanent display include *Americanoom* by Chryssa, *Le Neveu de Rameau* by Frank Stella, *Football Player* by Duane Hanson, *Modular Painting in Four Panels* by Roy Lichtenstein, *Portrait of Mrs Collins* by Thomas Gainsborough, and *Rex* by Deborah Butterfield.

8 Greco-Roman

Classical sculpture is represented by several marble carvings, including a Roman bust of a matron. The 6th-century BC black-figure krater depicting Artemis, Leto, and Apollo is noteworthy.

9 Renaissance and Baroque

The exquisite collection of mostly paintings includes works by Dosso Dossi, Tintoretto, Jordaens, Lucas Cranach the Elder, and Palma Vecchio.

10 African

The 16th-century cast bronze ring of the Yoruba people, depicting ritual decapitation, a Nok terracotta figure, and an Elpe or Ngbe society emblem assemblage all have an undeniable potency **(above)**.

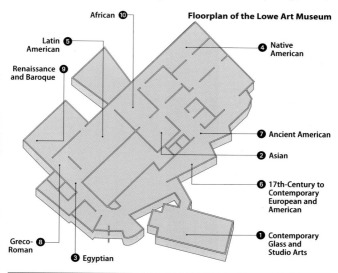

Floorplan of the Lowe Art Museum

African 🔟

Latin American ❺

Renaissance and Baroque ❾

Native American ❹

Ancient American ❼

Asian ❷

17th-Century to Contemporary European and American ❻

Contemporary Glass and Studio Arts ❶

Greco-Roman ❽

Egyptian ❸

NEED TO KNOW

MAP F3 ■ 1301 Stanford Drive ■ 305-284-3535 ■ www.lowemuseum.org

Open 10am–4pm Tue–Sat; noon–4pm Sun; closed Mon

Adm $12.50; concessions $8; under-12s free; first Tue of every month free

■ Check out the museum store for a wide selection of beautifully illustrated books dedicated to the Lowe collection.

■ A local favorite, the **Titanic Brewing Company** *(5813 Ponce de Leon Blvd, 305-667-2537)* serves up seafood, live music, and hand-crafted ale.

Museum Guide
The Lowe is located in the middle of the campus of the University of Miami, which is located in southern Coral Gables and is easily accessible by the Miami Metrorail – just follow the signs. There is no particular order in which you are expected to visit the collections. Keep in mind that several of the galleries are always given over to special temporary exhibitions and events.

TOP 10 ⭐ The Wolfsonian–FIU

The building began life in the 1920s as the Washington Storage Company – Miami's wealthier winter residents used to store their valuables here when they were away. Eventually, in 1986, businessman Mitchell Wolfson, Jr. decided to buy it outright as a home for his vast assemblage of the rich detritus of modernity. It opened to the public in 1995. Approximately 180,000 objects include decorative and propaganda art, furniture, and more.

1 Ceiling, Chandeliers, and Brackets
These unique decorative features **(above)** come from a 1920s Miami car showroom.

2 Art Deco Mailbox
To the left of the elevator is a wonderful 1929 Art Deco bronze mailbox, originally in New York Central Railroad Terminal, Buffalo.

3 The Wrestler
A symbol of The Wolfsonian–FIU **(left)**, this confronts visitors near the elevator. Its brawny, nude, life-sized form is made of aluminum, perhaps the classic metal of 20th-century modernity.

4 Harry Clarke Window
This literature-themed stained-glass window **(above)** was created in 1926–30 for the League of Nations' International Labor Organization in Geneva, Switzerland.

5 Entrance Hall

The massive ceiling supports reflect the Mediterranean Revival style of the facade and are original. So are the terra-cotta floors, the woodwork over the doors leading to the elevator vestibule, and the rough stucco walls. All of the ornamental cast stone was done by hand.

6 Bridge Tender's House

Standing just north of The Wolfsonian's entrance stands this remarkable 1939 building, a stainless-steel hexagonal structure that has been designed in the Art Moderne style.

NEED TO KNOW

MAP R4 ■ 1001 Washington Ave, Miami Beach ■ 305-531-1001 ■ www.wolfsonian.org

Open 10am–6pm Mon, Tue, Thu & Sat; 10am–9pm Fri; noon–6pm Sun; closed Wed and national holidays

Adm $12; concessions $8; under-6s free

■ Free tours are offered 6–9pm Fri. Private tours can be arranged by appointment.

■ The museum library and research center can be accessed by appointment only.

7 Fountain

Positioned under a skylight, the fountain **(left)** was made from an elaborate Deco window grille from the Norris Theater in Pennsylvania. Composed of over 200 gilded and glazed terra-cotta tiles, the richly floral decoration belies the careful geometrical structure of the piece.

8 Wooden Staircase

This fine piece of modern woodcraft is fashioned from pine and steel. It came from the Curtis Bok residence, Gulph Mills, Pennsylvania, designed by Wharton Esherick in 1935.

9 Temporary Exhibits

Much of the space is used for special exhibits exploring themes of the modern age. The Wolfsonian is a leading authority on propaganda art, showing how savvy designers have used the science of psychology to create highly persuasive images for businesses and governments.

ORIENTATION

The Wolfsonian–FIU is a museum and a design research institute. Three floors are offices and storage and are not normally open to the public. Your tour should begin outside, progress to the Entrance Hall, then up the back elevator to floors 5, 6, and 7.

Floorplan of The Wolfsonian–FIU

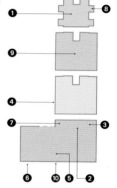

Key to Floorplan

■ First floor
■ Fifth floor
■ Sixth floor
■ Seventh floor

10 Mediterranean Revival Building

The Spanish Baroque-style relief around the main entrance **(above)** is a striking feature. The bronze flagpoles and finials date from 1914.

🔟 ⭐ Gold Coast Highway A1A

The best way to get a feel for the quality of life along the Gold Coast is to drive north on A1A. The road hugs the beach almost all the way and passes through beautiful natural settings and some of the wealthiest communities in the US. The 50-mile (80-km) route can be traversed in a day, but it's worth spending more time to take in the local color, from tropical nature preserves to fabulous mansions, all within sight of the sugary blond sands and the azure Atlantic.

Flagler Museum ①

This historic landmark **(right)** was Henry M. Flagler's *(see p39)* wedding gift to his third wife, Mary Lily Kenan, who was half his age and an heiress herself. The trappings of royalty are everywhere, down to the mid-18th century Louis XV commode.

② Norton Museum of Art

Perhaps Florida's finest museum of art, featuring over 7,000 Impressionist, Modern American, Chinese, and European works of art *(see p43)*.

③ The Breakers

This is the third hotel to be built on this site, the first two having burned down. The aura of America's Gilded Age (1880–1910) still clings to this stylish abode **(below)**, from the frescoed Italianate ceilings to the many crystal chandeliers *(see p148)*.

④ Las Olas Boulevard, Fort Lauderdale

Fort Lauderdale's main street has upscale shops and eateries. Las Olas Riverfront is a colorful mall, from which a river cruise departs.

⑤ Worth Avenue, Palm Beach

The street for local and visiting VIPs to select this week's wardrobe and perhaps a little *objet d'art*.

⑥ John U. Lloyd Beach State Park

This long barrier island commands views of busy Port Everglades and a beach historically significant as one designated for African-Americans in the days of segregation. It is now a destination popular with the LGBT+ community *(see p62)*.

7 Bonnet House

Built in 1920, this period home **(left)** is full of the personality of its creators, Frederic and Evelyn Bartlett. They were both artists, as is evident from the highly original murals and the somewhat eccentric tropical gardens.

8 Gumbo Limbo Nature Center

An informative center, with a boardwalk that winds through mangroves and hammocks (raised areas) in Red Reef Park. It takes its name from the gumbo limbo tree, which has distinctive, red peeling bark (see p55).

9 Atlantis Condominium

This 1980s monument appeared in the opening credits to *Miami Vice*, and in *Scarface*. It is famous for its cuboid, five-story palm court, a hole cut out of the building's facade which holds a Jacuzzi, a red spiral staircase, and a single palm tree (see p40).

ALL THAT GLITTERS

Here, all that glitters is probably gold! The Gold Coast may be named for the gold doubloons that Spanish galleons used to transport along the intracoastal waterways, but these days the term is used more for the golden lifestyle of the many millionaires and billionaires who have winter homes here.

Map of the Gold Coast Highway A1A

NEED TO KNOW

Flagler Museum: **MAP D2**; 1 Whitehall Way, Palm Beach; 561-655-2833

Norton Museum of Art: **MAP D2**; 1451 S. Olive Ave, West Palm Beach; 561-832-5196

Atlantis Condominium: **MAP M5**; 2025 Brickell Ave, Miami (just off the A1A)

■ Take the three-hour Jungle Queen Cruise *(954-462-5596)* to get the most out of Fort Lauderdale.

■ Have lunch in Fort Lauderdale at Noodles Panini *(821 East Las Olas Blvd, 954-462-1514)*. At dinnertime, head for Bistro Mezzaluna *(741 SE 17th St Causeway, 954-522-6620)*.

10 The Broadwalk

This famous stretch of Hollywood Beach **(above)** runs from South Sunset Road to Sheridan, where 2.5 miles (4 km) of shops, bars, and restaurants abound, serving the best of all the French-Caribbean fusion of Sugar Reef.

Key West

First recorded by Spanish explorers in 1513, this tiny island or key, measuring approximately 4 miles (6.5 km) in length and just about 2 miles (3 km) in width, has changed in status from a pirates' den to one of the most prosperous cities per capita in the United States. Always attracting free-thinkers, eccentrics, and misfits, Key West has a uniquely oddball character that is still apparent despite the upscale tourism industry that has developed since the 1990s. The island's self-named Conch (pronounced "konk") inhabitants include many writers, artists, and New-Agers.

1 Key West Museum of Art and History

Housed in the imposing old Customs House (above) are paintings of some of the island's eccentrics and notables, along with accounts of life here in various epochs.

2 Mallory Square

Every evening at sunset, the fun-loving citizens of the self-styled "Conch Republic" throw a party in this square, complete with entertainers.

3 Audubon House & Tropical Gardens

The house offers visitors a glimpse into mid-19th-century island life. The "ghosts" of the family who lived here take you on an audio tour through the impressive rooms.

4 Duval Street

The main street of Old Town (above) is the place to do the "Duval Crawl" – the arduous task of stopping in at all of the 100 or so bars, pubs, and clubs that line Duval Street and its neighboring roads.

5 The Hemingway Home

Ernest Hemingway lived from 1931 to 1940 in this Spanish colonial-style coral rock house (right). Remnants of his stay include the supposed descendants of his six-toed cats.

6 Key West Cemetery

The tombs are raised to avoid flooding as the soil is mostly hard coral rock. Droll epitaphs include "I told you I was sick" on the tomb of a hypochondriac.

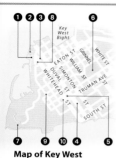

Map of Key West

8 Mel Fisher Maritime Museum

This engaging museum is dedicated to the lure and romance of sunken treasure and the equipment that has been used to retrieve it. Most impressive are the gold artifacts retrieved from 17th-century Spanish galleons *(see p122)*.

TOP 10 DENIZENS

1 Henry Flagler Standard Oil magnate
2 José Martí Cuban freedom fighter
3 John James Audubon Naturalist
4 Ernest Hemingway Writer
5 Harry S. Truman President
6 Tennessee Williams Playwright
7 Robert Frost Poet
8 John Dewey Educator-philosopher
9 Jimmy Buffett Singer-songwriter
10 Tallulah Bankhead Actress

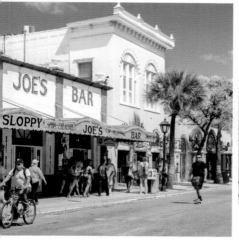

9 Bahama Village

An archway across Petronia Street **(above)** at Duval announces that you are entering this largely African-American neighborhood, which offers a tiny slice of Island culture. A block in is the Bahama Market, featuring handicrafts; farther along is the Blue Heaven restaurant.

7 Fort Zachary Taylor Historic State Park

The 1866 brick fort is now a military museum with a fine collection of Civil War artifacts.

NEED TO KNOW
MAP A6

Visitor Information: Chamber of Commerce, 510 Greene St ■ www.keywestchamber.org

Key West Museum of Art and History, Lighthouse Museum: open 9am–4:30pm daily; adm

Audubon House & Tropical Gardens: www.audubonhouse.com

The Hemingway Home: www.hemingwayhome.com

Key West Cemetery: open sunrise–6pm daily

Fort Zachary Taylor Historic State Park: open 8am–sunset daily; adm; www.floridastateparks.org

■ The Conch Tour Train is a must-do *(see p127)*.

■ Eat at Blue Heaven, the quintessence of old Key West *(see p131)*.

10 Lighthouse Museum

Built in 1845, Key West's lighthouse was capable of beaming light 25 miles (40 km) out to sea. Climb the 88 steps to enjoy panoramic seascapes and views of the town.

TOP 10 ★ The Everglades

Commanding one of the planet's most fascinating ecosystems, the Everglades is a vast, shallow river system of swamps and wetlands, where the waters can take a year or more to meander from the Kissimmee River, northwest of Miami, into Florida Bay. At least 45 plant varieties grow here that are found nowhere else on earth. It is also home to over 350 kinds of bird, 500 types of fish, and dozens of reptile and mammal species.

1 Big Cypress Swamp
This shallow wetland is a range of wet and dry habitats determined by slight differences in elevation. It is home to the Florida panther.

5 Corkscrew Swamp
A boardwalk **(right)** leads through various habitats, including old cypress full of nesting birds. The endangered wood stork has been seen here.

2 Anhinga and Gumbo Limbo Trails
Both these trails begin at the Royal Palm Visitor Center, the site of Florida's first state park **(above)**.

3 Ah-Tah-Thi-Ki and Billie Swamp
The Ah-Tah-Thi-Ki museum focuses on Seminole culture (see p42). Billie Swamp has exhilarating airboat rides and informative Buggy Eco-Tours, from which you might spot alligators.

6 Mahogany Hammock
Near Flamingo is one of the park's largest hammocks (fertile mounds), where a trail meanders through dense tropical growth. This is home to the largest mahogany tree in the country and colorful tree snails.

7 Fakahatchee Strand
This is one of Florida's wildest areas **(below)**, a 20-mile (32-km) slough (muddy backwater), noted for the largest stand of native royal palms in the US, unique air plants, and rare orchids. There are boardwalks and rangers on hand.

4 Shark Valley
This area, only 17 miles (27 km) from the western edge of Miami, has a 15-mile (24-km) loop road that you can travel by bicycle or on a narrated tram ride. It ends at a tower that affords great views.

8 Everglades National Park

The park features elevated boardwalks, tours, canoe rental **(above)**, camping, and accommodation.

PRESERVING THE EVERGLADES

The Everglades evolved over a period of more than six million years, but humans almost destroyed its fragile balance in less than 100. In the 1920s, the Hoover Dike closed off the area's main water source, Lake Okeechobee; Highway 41 further blocked its flow. Environmentalist Marjory Stoneman Douglas reversed the situation. Today, work continues slowly on building levees around the area to help keep the vital moisture in.

10 Flamingo

This outpost was badly damaged by Hurricane Irma in September 2017. However, sportfishing, camping, canoeing, bird-watching, and hiking are still possible. Repairs are underway to revive it.

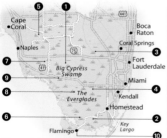

Map of the Everglades

9 Tamiami Trail (US 41)

This was the first road to open up the area by linking the Atlantic and Gulf coasts. It passes pioneer camps, such as Everglades City and Chokoloskee, which have barely changed since the late 1800s. They mark the western entrance to Everglades National Park.

NEED TO KNOW
MAPS C4

Big Cypress Swamp: Oasis Visitor Center; 239-695-1201

Royal Palm Visitor Center: 305-242-7237

Ah-Tah-Thi-Ki: 34725 W Boundary Rd, Clewiston; www.ahtahthiki.com

Billie Swamp: www.billieswamp.com

Shark Valley: 305-221-8776 (visitor center)

Corkscrew Swamp: 375 Sanctuary Rd; 239-348-9151

Fakahatchee Strand: 239-695-4593

Everglades National Park: 305-242-7700; www.nps.gov/ever

Flamingo: 239-695-2945 (visitor center)

■ Visit early, when many animals are active. Keep to the boardwalks.

The Top 10 of Everything

Diving by the submerged Christ of the Abyss statue, off Key Largo

ⓤ Historic Sites and Monuments

Coral Castle, a mysterious sculpture created by Edward Leedskalnin

1 Vizcaya Museum and Gardens

James Deering's opulent monument with its rich artistic traditions has become Miami's most beloved social and cultural center *(see pp20–21)*.

2 Ancient Spanish Monastery

Built in 1133–41 in Segovia, Spain, this monastic building was bought by William Randolph Hearst in 1925 and shipped to New York. The parts were reassembled here in 1952, though a few pieces were left over *(see p99)*.

3 Charles Deering Estate

James Deering's half-brother built this residence for himself. The original 19th-century house, Richmond Cottage, was destroyed by Hurricane Andrew in 1992 *(see p116)*.

4 Coral Gables Merrick House

The house where the Merrick family lived in the late 1800s and where George Merrick, Coral Gables' master builder, grew up. The contrast between the modest surroundings of his home and the spectacle of his grandiose dreams is fascinating *(see p111)*.

5 Coral Castle

This monument to unrequited love speaks volumes about early Florida's place in US history as a refuge for misfits, eccentrics, and visionaries. Land was cheap (the creator of Coral Castle bought his acre plot for $12 in 1920) and the population was sparse, so it was easy to do your own thing without being bothered. But how this gargantuan folly was actually constructed remains an enigma *(see p115)*.

6 Brigade 2506 Memorial

Little Havana's Eternal Flame and monument garden remembers those who died in the Bay of Pigs debacle, attempting to reclaim Cuba from leftist revolutionary forces in 1961 *(see p18)*.

7 Holocaust Memorial

MAP R2 ■ 1933–45 Meridian Ave, South Beach ■ 305-538-1663 ■ www.holocaustmmb.org

Miami has one of the largest populations of Holocaust survivors in the world, so this stunning monument has extra poignancy. Sculpted by

Bronze Holocaust Memorial

Kenneth Treister and finished in 1990, the centerpiece is a huge bronze forearm bearing a stamped number from Auschwitz. The arm is thronged with nearly 100 life-sized figures in attitudes of suffering. The surrounding plaza has a graphic pictorial history of the Holocaust, and a granite wall listing the names of thousands of concentration camp victims.

8 Opa-Locka
MAP G2 ▪ Cnr NW 27th Ave & NW 135th St

Despite the rather seamy area it inhabits, "The Baghdad of Dade County" is worth visiting for its 90 or so pink Moorish-style buildings. They were built here by Glenn Curtiss during the 1920s boom.

9 The Barnacle
Built in 1891, this is Dade County's oldest house, which cleverly uses ship-building techniques to make it stormproof as well as comfortable, allowing for Florida's steamy climate (see p108).

House at Barnacle Historic State Park

10 Stranahan House
MAP D3 ▪ 335 SE 6th Ave, near Las Olas ▪ 954-524-4736 ▪ Adm

Fort Lauderdale's oldest house was built originally in 1901 as a trading post for the Seminoles. The handsome two-story riverside house is furnished with period antiques, but it is the photos that best evoke the past, such as Stranahan trading alligator hides, otter pelts, and egret plumes with the local Seminoles. Such prizes were brought in from the Everglades in dugout canoes.

TOP 10 MOVERS AND SHAPERS

Marjory Stoneman Douglas

1 Marjory Stoneman Douglas
The first of Florida's environmentalists, who single-handedly saved the Everglades from development. She died in 1998, at the age of 108.

2 Henry M. Flagler
The legal mastermind (1830–1913) who opened up Florida through railroads and luxury construction.

3 Governor Napoleon Bonaparte Broward
Elected in 1905, he enacted Florida's first conservation laws and also a program for draining the Everglades.

4 Carl Fisher
An energetic developer in the early 1900s, Fisher was the first visionary owner of Miami Beach.

5 George Merrick
Merrick was the imaginative mind behind Coral Gables (see pp24–5).

6 The Deering Brothers
James (see pp20–21) and Charles (see p116) built homes that are now major attractions in Miami.

7 William Brickell
One of the first men to take advantage of the Homestead Act of 1862.

8 Barbara Baer Capitman
Capitman was the driving force behind the movement to save the area's Art Deco hotels (see p17).

9 Julia Tuttle
The dynamic pioneer who convinced Henry Flagler to extend his railroad down to Miami, in 1896.

10 Chief Jim Billie
This controversial Seminole chief was responsible for bringing wealth to his tribe in the 1980s, by building casinos on reservations.

🔟 Architectural Wonders

1 Art Deco District

A national treasure of uplifting architecture. In saving it, South Miami Beach not only transformed itself but also inspired a national movement to preserve historic struc- tures *(see pp14–17)*.

2 Atlantis Condominium

MAP M5 ▪ 2025 Brickell Ave, Miami

Built by Arquitectonica in 1982 and soon thereafter one of the stars of *Miami Vice*, this "building with the hole in it" is in danger of being overrun by the construction going on along Brickell. The "hole" is an ingenious 37-ft (11-m) cube cut out of the building's center, at the 12th floor. A red spiral staircase and a palm tree draw your attention to it in a delightful way.

3 Biltmore Hotel and Coral Gables Congregational Church

Facing each other across manicured gardens, these two structures are the heart of George Merrick's contribution to "the City Beautiful" *(see pp24–5)*.

Coral Gables Congregational Church

4 Freedom Tower

Inspired by the famous belfry of Seville's vast cathedral, La Giralda, which was formerly a minaret to the mosque that stood on the site under Almohad rule *(see p90)*.

Freedom Tower, a city landmark

5 Fontainebleau Hotel

Designed by architect Morris Lapidus, this landmark defines the Miami Modern Architecture (MiMo) style: sweeping lines, lots of colors, and inlaid marble floors with the Lapidus trademark bow- tie motif *(see p150)*.

6 Ingraham Building

MAP N2 ▪ 25 SE 2nd Ave, at Flagler St, Downtown

This Renaissance-Revival beauty is a don't-miss landmark, and it evokes all the glamour of the 1920s boom era.

7 Estefan Enterprises

MAP R5 ▪ 420 Jefferson Ave, Miami Beach

This playful building takes the frivolity of Deco several steps further. A free-form green-wave tower slices through a cool blue cube, evoking both sea and sky.

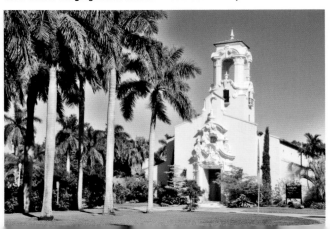

8 1111 Lincoln Road
MAP Q2 ▪ 1111 Lincoln Rd, at Alton Rd, South Beach

Dubbed "the most famous parking garage in the world," this unique open-air structure, completed in 2010 by Swiss architectural firm Herzog & de Meuron, looks like a precarious stack of cards.

9 Miami Tower
I. M. Pei's striking take on the ziggurat theme, so often used in Art Deco, looks for all the world like a stepped stack of CDs in various sizes. It is especially appealing at night when lit up with vibrant colors *(see p92)*.

The Miami Tower lit up at dusk

10 Key West Old Town
This small island *(see pp32–3)* has the US's largest collection of 19th-century structures. About 4,000 buildings, mostly houses, embody the distinctive local style. Many architectural features take their cues from elements used on ships, such as roof hatches to allow air circulation. A unique innovation is the "eyebrow" house, with second-floor windows hidden under a front porch roof overhang, providing shade in the heat.

TOP 10 MURALS AND MOSAICS

Mural, Little Havana

1 Little Havana
Calle Ocho 1507–13
A series of seven quirky murals decorate the Little Havana streets.

2 The Netherland
1330 Ocean Drive, South Beach
A fantastic mural of indolent sunbathers.

3 Bacardi Import Headquarters
2100 Biscayne Blvd
Don't miss the tropical foliage mosaic, and note the building next to it, too.

4 Miami Beach Post Office
1300 Washington Ave, South Beach
The classy Deco entrance to the post office has a triptych mural of Ponce de Leon and the Native American peoples.

5 Coral Gables City Hall
405 Biltmore Way
Denman Fink created the mural on the bell tower of this structure. The one above the stairs is by John St. John.

6 Buick Building
3841 NE 2nd Ave
Murals adorn the Brick Building's east and west walls. While there, enjoy the amazing public art in the Design District.

7 Office Building
1617 Drexel Ave, South Beach
A 1940s mural here depicts labor, the arts, and the universe.

8 The Society of the Four Arts
Four Arts Plaza, Palm Beach
See allegorical murals from 1939.

9 Wyland Whaling Walls
201 William St, Key West
An undersea world of whales and other cetaceans is featured here.

10 Bahama Village
Thomas St at Petronia St
A charming mural evokes daily life in the Bahama Village neighborhood.

🔟 Museums

Birds of America exhibition displayed at the HistoryMiami museum

1 HistoryMiami
MAP M2 ■ 101 West Flagler St ■ 305-375-1492 ■ Open 10am–5pm Tue–Sat, noon–5pm Sun; closed Mon ■ Adm ■ www.historymiami.org

Starting as far back in prehistory as 12,000 years, the museum slips swiftly through the millennia to reach Spanish colonization, Seminole culture, extravagance in the "Roaring Twenties," and Cuban immigration in more recent years.

2 Jewish Museum of Florida
With its stained-glass windows and Deco details, the former synagogue itself is as fascinating as the exhibits

Modern design, The Wolfsonian–FIU

it houses. The museum is dedicated to telling the story of the 230-year Jewish presence in Florida (see p83).

3 The Wolfsonian–FIU
The perfect complement to the Art Deco District, this museum and design research institute has a wealth of modern design exhibits (see pp28–9).

4 World Erotic Art Museum
MAP R4 ■ Mezzanine level 1205 Washington Ave ■ 305-532-9336 ■ Open 11am–10pm Mon–Thu, 11am–midnight Fri–Sun ■ Adm ■ www.weam.com

An astonishing $10 million collection of erotic art from around the world.

Jewish Museum of Florida building

5 Ah-Tah-Thi-Ki Seminole Indian Museum
This excellent museum, on the Big Cypress Indian Reservation, features Seminole artifacts, such as pottery and beautiful clothing. The Green Corn Ceremony is also explained, including the games, music, dance, and costumes involved. A nature trail leads through the cypress canopy, where signs explain the use of certain flora in Seminole culture (see p34).

6 Mel Fisher Maritime Museum

Immerse yourself in the romance of long-lost, booty-laden shipwrecks at this fascinating museum (see p122).

7 Cubaocho Museum

Learn more about Little Havana's history and culture at this small, yet informative, museum and art gallery. Cuban culture has been a key factor in Miami's identity since the 1950s, a legacy explored through revolving exhibits of Cuban art, an old-fashioned café, a bar serving stellar mojitos and live Cuban arts performances (see p93).

8 Lowe Art Museum

This is undoubtedly Miami's top art museum, featuring works from European, American, Chinese, Pre-Columbian, and Native American cultures (see pp26–7).

9 Norton Museum of Art

One of South Florida's finest museums. Its European collection displays works by Rembrandt, Goya, Renoir, and Picasso. Americans include O'Keeffe and Pollock, and the museum also has photography and contemporary art (see p30).

Entrance to Pérez Art Museum Miami

10 Pérez Art Museum Miami

Besides impressive temporary shows, the museum's permanent collection focuses on art since the 1940s, and includes works by Frankenthaler, Gottlieb, Rauschenberg, and Stella. It's set in lovely gardens (see p91).

TOP 10 CONTEMPORARY COLLECTIONS

Wynwood Walls graffiti

1 Wynwood Walls
2528 NW 2nd Ave
A cutting-edge project brings the world's greatest graffiti artists to Miami.

2 Margulies Collection
591 NW 27th Ave
Important photography collection, favoring straightforward portraiture.

3 Gallery Diet
6315 NW 2nd Ave
An ever-changing space where emerging and mid-career artists shine.

4 Kevin Bruk Gallery, Miami
2249 NW 1st Place
Features work by New York artists Max Gimblett and John Yau.

5 Bernice Steinbaum Gallery, Miami
2101 Tigertail Ave
The work of Edouard Duval Carrie and Wendy Wischer.

6 Artspace/Virginia Miller Galleries
169 Madeira Ave, Coral Gables
International fine art, including paintings and photography.

7 Locust Projects
3852 N Miami Ave
Specializing in computer-aided and video work by local artists.

8 Rubell Family Collection
95 NW 29th St
About 1,000 works by modern artists, including Haring, Koons, Basquiat, and Cuban artist José Bedia.

9 Cernuda Arte
3155 Ponce de Leon Blvd, Coral Gables
Cuban art from all periods.

10 Fredric Snitzer Gallery
1540 NE Miami Ct
New collage paintings, featuring the work of Sandy Winters.

Parks, Gardens, and Zoos

1 Flamingo Gardens

MAP D3 ■ 3750 South Flamingo Rd, Davie/Fort Lauderdale ■ Adm ■ www.flamingogardens.org

These beautiful gardens began life in 1927 as a weekend retreat for the citrus-farming Wray family. The lush botanical gardens and wildlife and bird sanctuary are worth at least half a day. There's a "free-flight" aviary, featuring a mass of Florida birds, including the comical roseate spoonbill and, of course, the flamingo. The rare bald eagle has also made a home here.

Flamingo Gardens resident

2 Pinecrest Gardens

This thoroughly enjoyable place features over 1,000 kinds of tropical plants, an art gallery, and an amphitheater for concerts and shows. There are also plenty of activities here for children (see p58).

3 Fairchild Tropical Botanic Garden

One of the best of South Florida's ravishing tropical gardens dotted with man-made lakes and a large collection of rare plants (see p115).

Fairchild Tropical Botanic Garden

4 Safari Edventure

This wildlife park, in the southwest suburbs of Miami, specializes in hands-on wildlife experiences suitable for the whole family. Interact with over 100 species of wildlife (see p115).

5 Morikami Museum and Japanese Gardens

MAP D3 ■ 4000 Morikami Park Road, Delray Beach ■ 561-495-0233 ■ Adm ■ www.morikami.org

Blossoming from a Japanese colony founded here in 1905, the Yamato-kan villa is surrounded by formal Japanese gardens of various ages: a Heian (9th- to 12th-century) *shinden*-style garden, a paradise garden emulating those of the 13th–14th centuries, rock gardens, a flat garden, and a modern romantic garden. This is a tranquil sanctuary in the midst of bustling South Florida.

6 Lion Country Safari

MAP C2 ■ 2003 Lion Country Safari Road, Loxahatchee ■ 561-793-1084 ■ Adm ■ www.lioncountrysafari.com

Besides recreations of habitats in Kenya, Zimbabwe, Mozambique, the

Kalahari, and the Serengeti, the extensive park also features giraffe-feeding and a petting zoo. Drive or take a guided bus tour through over 500 acres (200 ha) of wildlife.

7 Fruit & Spice Park

Located in the Redland District south of Coconut Grove, this is the only tropical botanical garden of its kind in the United States. The exotic plants are grouped by country of origin, and the tropical climate here sustains over 100 varieties of citrus plant, 65 of banana, and 40 of grape. The vast, lush park also houses the largest bamboo collection in the US. In the gift store you'll find imported fruit products, including dried and canned fruit, juices, jams, teas, and unusual seeds (see p115).

Crop display at the Fruit & Spice Park

8 Montgomery Botanical Center

This nonprofit botanical center, accessible by appointment only, holds a vast collection of exotic plants from across the globe (see p115).

9 Nancy Forrester's Secret Garden

MAP A6 ▪ 518 Elizabeth Street, Key West ▪ 305-294-0015 ▪ Adm

Lose yourself in this impossibly lush acre of land just a block off Duval Street. Intensely beautiful, the garden exudes a sense of peace and contentment. The ravishing varieties of flora – orchids, bromeliads, rare palms – and the well-loved parrots put any visitor at ease.

10 Zoo Miami

This extremely well-conceived and beautifully maintained animal park is divided into habitats that imitate Australasia, Asia, and Africa. It is the largest zoological park in Florida, covering nearly 750 acres (304 ha), and it takes at least three hours to walk around it all (the time is well worth spending). If you prefer, take the 45-minute tram tour or Zoofari monorail for a nominal additional charge. Animals include jaguars, tigers, African elephants, anacondas, and giant river otters. There are many feeding and animal encounter attractions that give endless delight to children (see p116).

Giraffe-feeding at Zoo Miami

🔟 Romantic Spots

Gardens adorned with water features of carved stone, Vizcaya Museum

1 Vizcaya Museum and Gardens

This is a glorious pastiche of styles from more or less 500 years of European architecture. Most of it was bought in the Old World by an early-20th-century farm machinery magnate to be remodeled into this comfortable palace, surrounded by enchanting gardens (see pp20–21).

2 Coral Castle

One lovesick Latvian immigrant, Edward Leedskalnin, created this huge coral rock Valentine heart to win back his fickle love. The woman

remained unmoved by his Herculean labors, however, and he died here alone in 1951 (see p115).

3 Fairchild Tropical Botanic Garden

The tranquil, silvery lakes, fragrant, shaded bowers, and lush, dappled retreats are capable of bringing out the romantic in anyone. Explore at your own pace, or take it all in with the 40-minute tram tour – and perhaps stay for dinner at the nearby Red Fish Grill (see p115).

4 Ancient Spanish Monastery Cloister and Gardens

With its magnificent gardens and cloisters redolent of ancient lands and courtly love, this has become a popular spot for weddings. The building can be traced back to 12th-century Spain, though it didn't make its way to Florida until the 20th century. Having lain dormant in packing crates for years, it was finally reassembled in the 1950s (see p99).

5 Venetian Pool

A lush fantasy of sculpted stone, water, and gardens, where Esther Williams (the bathing-beauty diva of yesteryear) used to star in synchronized swimming movies. The pool was born of the mind of entrepreneur George Merrick (see p24).

6 Morikami Japanese Gardens

The 1,000-year-old originals of some of these deeply peaceful settings were designed for Japanese nobility – places of inspiration for them to recite poetry to each other, or to seek solace in troubled times. Few places evoke the serenity and spiritual depth you can sense here, in the silent rocks and the murmuring cascades *(see p44)*.

7 Hotel St. Michel

French-style boutique hotel with an exquisite restaurant. Stay a night or two and you'll think you're in a chic little pension in Paris. The subtly lit bistro is a perfect place for a quietly intimate tête-à-tête, yet all this is within walking distance of downtown Coral Gables *(see pp151)*.

8 Key Biscayne Lighthouse

MAP H4 ▪ 1200 S Crandon Blvd, Key Biscayne ▪ 305 361 5811 ▪ Open 9am–4pm Thu–Mon ▪ www.floridastateparks.org/park/ Cape-Florida

Bill Baggs Cape Florida State Park contains this historic lighthouse,

which was built in 1825 and soars 95 ft (29 m) into the sky. As the surrounding beaches and scrub are completely untouched, climbing the 109 steps affords mesmerizing views; it's a popular spot for loved-up couples who come here to propose.

Watching the sunset, Mallory Square

9 Mallory Square, Key West, at Sunset

Although you will most likely be there with a hoard of other sunset-viewers, the beauty of this moment and the general air of merriment will provide you with a memorable experience. Watch tall ships sail in front of the huge setting sun, blazing orangy-pink at the Gulf's edge. True romantics should keep an eye out for the beguiling green flash that's said to occur just before the sun disappears below the horizon – if you catch it, it means good luck in love *(see p32)*.

10 Red Fish Grill

Perhaps the most starry-eyed setting in Miami, with its shimmering bay views and evocatively lit foliage. The potent backdrop of Biscayne Bay, Fairchild Tropical Botanic Gardens, and nearby Mattheson Hammock Park and saltwater Atoll Pool make this an unforgettable place to dine. Attentive service and delicious food complete the experience *(see p119)*.

Key Biscayne Lighthouse

🔟 Spots for People-Watching

A late-night gathering at Clevelander

1 Clevelander

This hotel's beachfront cafés evolve into one of SoBe's top pool-bar scenes after dark. Its proximity to the beach inspires a casual style, and there's always a crowd to enjoy happy hour and live music *(see p88)*.

2 Ocean Drive

The epitome of the "American Riviera." Sit in a café, or cruise up and down in a convertible, on skates, or simply on foot. And if you've got it – the buff bod, golden tan – Ocean Drive is the place to show it off *(see p13)*.

3 Bayside Marketplace

There is never a dull moment in Downtown Miami's hottest day-time spot, which features a variety of boutiques, live music, street performers, and ethnic dining right on the marina *(see p92)*.

4 Lincoln Road Mall

Second only to Ocean Drive in its star-quality appeal. Lined with sculpture-fountains and plants, this pedestrian area with its outdoor eateries is always lively *(see p82)*.

5 La Marea at the Tides

Try the famous Tropical Popsicle Martini as you watch the people go by. La Marea is popular with celebrities, so look around – you might be dining side by side with the rich and famous *(see p88)*.

6 The Forge Restaurant and Winebar

Established in 1968, this restaurant and wine bar is one of Miami's legendary institutions and a perennial favorite with celebrities. The famous and award-winning "Super Steak" is a Forge classic, but chef Dewey LoSasso also serves up less conventional fare, including the lobster, peanut butter, and jelly

Famous Art Deco architecture along fashionable Ocean Drive

sandwich. The eight-room wine cellar, which is arranged by flavor, is formidable *(see p89)*.

7 Commodore Plaza

Coconut Grove's second most frequented spot is this intersection, where every corner features a top viewing position for the constant circulation of pedestrian traffic, everyone scoping out a café or restaurant, and each other. Try the Green Street Café *(see p110)*.

8 Hollywood Broadwalk

The Broadwalk is a rare swath of beach where a 2.5-mile (4-km) pedestrian walkway fronts directly on to the sand, just to the north of Miami Beach. It's non-stop surfside fun, with loads of revelers of all kinds cruising up and down *(see p31)*.

Popular at sunset, Mallory Square

9 Mallory Square, Key West

Especially at sunset, this huge Key West square at the Gulf end of Duval Street is a gathering place for all kinds of locals and visitors. Street performers keep it lively, and there are plenty of vendors of food and souvenirs *(see p32)*.

10 CocoWalk

A host of select restaurants, outdoor cafés, shops, and a cineplex provides the entertainment. But, here in the heart of the Grove, it's great just to hang out and listen to the live band playing, most of the time, on the balcony above *(see p107)*.

TOP 10 TRENDY CAFÉS

News Café on Ocean Drive

1 News Café
Justifiably SoBe's most famous café, in a prime spot on Ocean Drive *(see p88)*.

2 Raleigh Miami Beach
This classy hotel's European-style coffee bar is a particular favorite among visiting celebrities *(see p150)*.

3 Green Street Café
Coconut Grove's numero uno for people-watching, happy hour, and creative meals *(see p110)*.

4 Berries in the Grove
Sit outdoors or on the patio to really get the most out of happy hour, lunch, and brunch especially *(see p113)*.

5 Nexxt Café
Diners at Nexxt Café can be found munching on huge entrées and sipping colorful cocktails at any time of day, while people-watching from the umbrella tables *(see p88)*.

6 Mango's Tropical Café
One of the hottest action venues on South Beach, where you can enjoy live music and dancing, Floribbean dishes, and free-flowing cocktails *(see p88)*.

7 The Clay
This beautiful period building has been transformed into a youth hostel, so its modest café is always thronged with international youth *(see p153)*.

8 Books and Books
Don't let the quietness deceive you; this is a very happening place *(see p112)*.

9 La Marea at the Tides
Soak up the romantic atmosphere at the outside tables facing the ocean in trendy South Beach *(see p88)*.

10 Mangoes, Key West
A restaurant, bar, and sidewalk café, located on a busy corner *(see p131)*.

🔟 Beaches

1 Bill Baggs Cape Florida State Park

Home to a historic 19th-century lighthouse, this pristine beach is located at the southern tip of Key Biscayne *(see p82)*.

2 Crandon Park

One of several South Florida beaches rated among the top ten in the US, this one is on upper Key Biscayne *(see p82)*.

Beautiful Crandon Park Beach

3 South Pointe Park Beach
MAP S6

Though not well known for its beaches, South Pointe Park's northern part is frequented by surfers, and you can watch cruise ships gliding in and out of the Port of Miami. It's also great for walks, and there's a fitness course, an observation tower, charcoal grills, picnic spots, and playgrounds.

4 Bahia Honda State Park

Frequently voted the best beach in the US, Bahia Honda is celebrated for its perfect white sands, great watersports, and exotic tropical forests *(see p121)*.

5 Key West Beaches
MAP A6

Key West's relatively modest beaches are strung out along the southern side of the island, stretching from Fort Zachary Taylor Historic State Park in the west to Smathers Beach in the east. The latter is the largest and most popular, but locals favor the former because it's less crowded. For convenience, the beach at the bottom of Duval Street, at the Southernmost Point in the US, is fine, friendly, and offers several good refreshment options.

6 Hobie Island Beach and Virginia Key Beach
MAP H3

While Hobie beach is popular with windsurfers, Virginia Key – neighbor to Key Biscayne and similarly shrouded in Australian pines – has no residents and few visitors. Under Old South segregation, it was the only Miami beach African-Americans were allowed to use. Once you walk through the vegetation, the 2-mile (3-km) beach here is fine and relatively empty. Both are excellent for children due to the warm bay waters, but Virginia Key has deep waters and possible undertow.

rocky sand, this developing strip is popular with older tourists, as well as surfers and sailors. Souvenir shops and hotels indulge in striking architectural fancies, featuring exotic themes, along Collins (A1A) between 157th and 193rd streets *(see p99)*.

⑨ Haulover Park Beach
MAP H1

Located just north of Bal Harbour, Haulover has been spared the sight of high-rise development. Noted for its clear blue waters, the dune-backed beach lies along the eastern side of the park. To the north is a clothing optional stretch – the only nude beach in the county.

⑩ Matheson Hammock Park Beach
MAP G4

North of Fairchild Tropical Botanic Garden, this beautiful 100-acre (40-ha) park was developed in the 1930s by Commodore J. W. Matheson. It features the man-made Atoll Pool, a saltwater swimming pool encircled by sand and palm trees and flushed naturally by nearby Biscayne Bay. The tranquil beach is popular with families and enjoys warm, safe waters surrounded by tropical hardwood forests. Other attractions include walking trails through the mangrove swamp.

Matheson Hammock Park Beach

Aerial vista of Lummus Park Beach

⑦ Lummus Park Beach
MAP S3

This stretch of sand – broad, long, and well-maintained – is, for many, the epitome of South Beach. In season, you'll see bronzed bodies lined up row after row, some with boom boxes blasting, others just catching the rays. The more active play volleyball, do gymnastics, and, of course, take to the waves. On the stretch from 5th to 11th streets, women are allowed to go topless.

⑧ Sunny Isles Beach
More noteworthy for its 1950s tourist-resort kitsch than for its

🔟 Sports and Outdoor Activities

Men playing beach volleyball

1 Volleyball
On every beach in South Florida, you'll find volleyball nets and likely team members ready to go. This is the quintessential beach sport, where taking a tumble in the sand is part of the fun *(see p84)*.

2 In-line Skating
Gliding along on little wheels is probably the number one activity for the perennially tanned of South Florida. Down on flaunt-it-all South Beach, you can rent in-line skates or get fitted for your very own pair.

3 Golf
There are endless opportunities to play golf throughout South Florida, making it a premier golfing-holiday destination. Many larger resorts have their own courses, too, but one of the best in the Greater Miami area is Crandon Golf Course, which is the only public course on Key Biscayne *(see p84)*.

4 Cycling
This is an excellent way to explore South Beach, Key Biscayne, or Key West. Rental shops abound, and there are a good number of excellent bike trails in the Everglades, too *(see p84)*.

5 Fishing
Reward Fishing Fleet: www.therewardfleet.com ■ AWS Charters: keywestflatsfishin.com ■ Blue Waters Charter Key West: www.bwckeywest.com ■ Fishing Headquarters: www.fishheadquarters.com

There are any number of companies that will organize deep-sea fishing excursions; for good freshwater fishing you should head to Amelia Earhart Park or Lake Okeechobee.

6 Swimming
Miami and the Keys are home to some of the most beautiful beaches in the US. Head to Bahia Honda State Park *(see p121)* for pristine sandy beaches where you can enjoy the warm, clear blue waters of the Atlantic Ocean and Florida Bay.

7 Surfing and Windsurfing
Miami has good prevailing winds and both calm and surging waters – so there is plenty of scope for good surfing and windsurfing *(see p84)*. The Keys tend to be good for windsurfing only, as the surrounding reefs break the big waves *(see p126)*.

8 Tennis
South Floridians love this game, and there are public and

private courts everywhere. Key Biscayne is the top choice, of course, which is where the Sony Open is held every March *(see p84)*.

9 Jet-Skiing and Parasailing

Parawest: parawestparasailing.com ■ Sebago Watersports: keywest sebago.com ■ Fury Water Adventures: www.furycat.com

Not as challenging as they may appear and, of course, great fun. In Miami, the placid intracoastal waterways are suitable for both, but it's the Keys that have the best conditions for these adventure sports, especially Key West *(see p126)*.

Kayaking around the Keys

10 Boating and Kayaking

Blue Planet Kayak: 305-294-8087; www.blue-planet-kayak.com

Strike out on your own in a kayak and explore the colorful waters around the Keys, or the winding mangrove creeks off Florida Bay. Alternatively, you could enjoy an ecotour of the diverse marine life. Be sure to bring your camera along.

Teeing off, Crandon Golf Course

TOP 10 SPECTATOR SPORTS

Horse and jockey out on the track

1 Horse Racing
Gulfstream Park, 901 S Federal Hwy, Hallandale, Jan–Apr; Calder Race Course 21001 NW27th Ave, May–Dec
Two of the best places are Gulfstream Park, and Calder Race Course.

2 Jai Alai
Casino Miami, 3500 NW 37th Ave
Often called the world's fastest game.

3 Football
Hard Rock Stadium, 2269 NW 199th St
Miami's contender in the National Football League is the Miami Dolphins.

4 Dog Racing
Flagler Dog Track, 450 NW 37th Ave
While running greyhound races part of the year, Flagler has year-round simulcasting of dog and horse races.

5 Stock-Car Racing
1 Speedway Blvd
Homestead Miami Speedway hosts several big events every year.

6 Tennis
Crandon Park, Key Biscayne
The Sony Open is one of the world's biggest non-Grand Slam tournaments.

7 Polo
3667 120th Ave S, Wellington
Well represented in Palm Beach County.

8 Basketball
601 Biscayne Blvd
The Miami Heat calls the AmericanAirlines Arena home.

9 Ice Hockey
1 Panther Parkway, Sunrise
Local team the Florida Panthers play out by the Everglades.

10 Baseball
501 Marlins Way
Two-time world champions Miami Marlins play at Marlins Park.

TOP 10 Snorkeling and Diving

3 Biscayne National Underwater Park

Closer to Miami than John Pennekamp, this location has almost as many good snorkeling possibilities. You'll find vivid coral reefs to dive among, and mangrove swamps to explore by canoe (see p116).

4 Key Biscayne Parks

Both Crandon and Bill Baggs Parks have great areas for snorkeling, in some of Miami's cleanest, clearest waters (see p82).

1 Looe Key National Marine Sanctuary

This is a brilliant coral dive location, and the closest great snorkeling to Key West. Access from Bahia Honda State Park (see p121).

2 John Pennekamp Coral Reef State Park

This park offers some of the best snorkeling in the world. Boats can also be rented here, or you can take a glass-bottomed boat (see p121).

The beach at Fort Zachary Taylor

5 Key West Waters
MAP A6

Take the plunge right off the beach at Fort Zachary Taylor Historic State Park, or join an expedition out to the reefs that lie around this island (see pp32–3). Plenty of trips are offered by local companies, most of them taking three to four hours in total, including at least an hour and a half of reef time. They usually leave twice a day, at around 9am and again around 1pm.

6 Bahia Honda State Park Waters

The beautiful, sandy beach of Bahia Honda in the Keys – often lauded as one of the best beaches in the US – has excellent waters for swimming and snorkeling. Equipment rentals are available here (see p121).

Statue, John Pennekamp Coral Reef

7 Red Reef Park
**Gumbo Limbo Nature Center:
MAP D3; 1801 North Ocean Blvd,
Boca Raton; 561-544-8605; open
9am–4pm Mon–Sat, noon–4pm Sun;
www.gumbolimbo.org**

Boca Raton is famous for its extensive
and beautifully maintained parks, and
this offers some of the area's best
beaches and snorkeling. An artificial
reef can provide hours of undersea
viewing and is suitable for young-
sters. The Gumbo Limbo Nature
Center is just across the street.

8 Islamorada
MAP C5

Halfway along the Keys, Islamorada
is a superb base for snorkeling and
diving trips. The nearby Crocker
and Alligator reefs provide habitats
for a wide variety of marine life.
The shipwrecks of the *Eagle* and the
Cannabis Cruiser are home to gar-
gantuan amberjack and grouper.

9 Dry Tortugas National Park

Found about 70 miles (110 km) west
of Key West, these seven islands
and their surrounding waters make a
fantastic park. The snorkeling sights
are exceptional, due to the shallow
waters and abundance of marine
life. You can snorkel directly off the
beaches of Fort Jefferson or take a
trip to the wreck of the *Windjammer*,
which sank on Loggerhead Reef in
1907. Tropical fish, goliath grouper,
and lobster can be spotted *(see p133)*.

Diving in waters off Fort Lauderdale

10 Fort Lauderdale Waters
**Sea Experience: MAP D3; 954-
770-3483; www.seaxp.com**

Fort Lauderdale has been awarded
the Blue Wave Beaches certification
for spotless sands and crystal clear
waters, which add up to superior
underwater viewing. Many of the
most interesting parts of the three-
tiered natural reef system here are
close to the shore, although most
require a short boat ride. In addition,
more than 80 artificial reefs have
been built to enhance the growth
of marine flora and fauna. Sea
Experience is just one of several
companies organizing snorkeling
and scuba trips off this coastline.

The 19th-century Fort Jefferson on Garden Key, Dry Tortugas National Park

🔟 Off the Beaten Path

View out to sea from the Kampong

1 The Kampong
One of Miami's lesser-visited gems, this tropical garden is sited southwest of downtown Coconut Grove. The former estate of horticulturalist David Fairchild, it holds an impressive collection of tropical flowers, fruit trees, and plants *(see p109)*.

2 Ermita de la Caridad Church, Coconut Grove
MAP M5 ▪ 3609 S Miami Ave, Coconut Grove ▪ 305-854-2404 ▪ Open 8am–9pm

Built in the late 1960s, this peculiar conical church is the religious heart of expat Cuban life. Beneath the altar there's a cache of Cuban soil and sand, salvaged from a refugee boat, while above it a mural depicts the history of the Catholic Church in Cuba. The shrine is dedicated to Our Lady of Charity, the Cuban patron saint (the statue inside is a replica of the revered original from the shrine in El Cobre).

3 Los Pinareños Fruteria
This fruit stand and outdoor café in the heart of Little Havana seems transported straight from Cuba. Afro-Cuban tunes waft through boxes of papaya, oranges, guavas, and coconuts, while plates of delicious chicken rice and fresh juices are doled out from the kitchen *(see p96)*.

4 Overtown
MAP G3 ▪ Lyric Theater 819 NW 2nd Ave ▪ 786-708-4610 ▪ www.bahlt.org

Miami's black community thrived in this segregated neighborhood after the incorporation of the city in 1896. Remnants of the area's glory days include the beautifully renovated Lyric Theater, opened in 1913. It acts as a cultural center today, home to the Black Archives museum.

5 Santería & Vodou Botánicas
This is South Florida at its most darkly exotic. The *botánicas* (traditional folk medicine shops) in Little Haiti carry

Ermita de la Caridad Church

all sorts of potions, candles, gaudy statuary, and glass jars packed with herbs used in the practice of the hybrid Caribbean religions of *Santería* and Vodou (Voodoo) – Roman Catholicism blended with ancient West African ritual and belief *(see p19)*.

6 Ancient Spanish Monastery

MAP H1 ■ 16711 W Dixie Hwy, North Miami Beach ■ 305-945-1461

Built in 1133 near Segovia, this monastery was occupied by Cistercian monks for almost 700 years. In 1925 it was aquired by the publisher William Randolph Hearst, who had the building shipped to the US in more than 11,000 crates. The structure languished in warehouse until it was bought by the Episcopalian church in 1964. Today it serves a growing congregation and attracts many visitors.

7 Nancy Forrester's Secret Garden, Key West

Local artist Nancy Forrester and her friends began working on this lush, funky, and indefinable Key West garden in the 1970s *(see p45)*.

8 Opa-Locka

This neighborhood, offering yet another delightful example of Miami's quirky fantasy architecture, was dreamed up by Glenn Curtiss in the 1920s. Be vigilant in the rather rundown district around it *(see p39)*.

9 Stiltsville, Key Biscayne

MAP H4

■ www.stiltsvilletrust.org

Drive to the southernmost tip of Key Biscayne, look way out over the water, and you'll spy seven fragile-looking structures built on stilts. These fishermen's bungalows are the last of what was once a much larger community from the 1930s to 1960s. Their number has dwindled due to hurricanes, and the site is now overseen by the Stiltsville Trust (public access is by permit only).

Wooden house out at sea, Stiltsville

10 "The Garden of Eden," Key West

MAP A6 ■ The Bull and Whistle Bar, 3/F, 224 Duval St, Key West ■ 305-296-4565 ■ Open noon–3am daily ■ www.bullkeywest.org

Devoted nudists can find an appreciative milieu in this renowned bar *(see p130)*, as well as within the walls and gardens of many guesthouses scattered around town.

🔟 Children's Attractions

1 The Key West Butterfly and Nature Conservatory

MAP A6 ■ 1316 Duval Street, Key West 33040 ■ 305-296-2988 ■ Open 9am–5pm daily ■ Adm ■ www.keywestbutterfly.com

Take a magical stroll through the exotic conservatory filled with hundreds of beautiful butterflies, flowering plants, trees, birds, and cascading waterfalls in this climate-controlled, glass-enclosed habitat.

2 Pinecrest Gardens

MAP F4 ■ 11000 Red Road, Pinecrest ■ Open 10am–5pm Mon–Fri, 9am–5pm Sat & Sun ■ Adm ■ www.pinecrestgardens.org

There's plenty for kids to enjoy here: a Splash N Play area, petting zoo, colourful playground, domino games, and a giant chess and checkers board, along with children's theater performances, concerts, and movies.

Facade of Miami Children's Museum

3 Miami Children's Museum

MAP G3 ■ 980 MacArthur Causeway ■ 305-373-5437 ■ Open 10am–6pm daily ■ Adm ■ www.miamichildrens museum.org

Play, learn, imagine, and create at this museum. Interactive exhibits related to the arts, culture, and communication are on offer. Catch a fish in the waterfall or take a trip on a pretend cruise ship complete with portholes.

4 Amelia Earhart Park

MAP G2 ■ 401 E 65th St, at NW 42nd Ave ■ 305-685-8389 ■ Open 9am–sunset daily ■ Adm

Come to this park for a fun and wholesome family day out. There's a petting zoo with lots of baby animals to see and pony rides on weekends, islands to search out, beaches to explore, playgrounds, and fish-filled lakes. Blacksmiths and craftsmen demonstrate their skills, and the whole park is delightfully uncrowded, as it is well away from the tourist track.

5 Key West Aquarium

MAP A6 ■ 1 Whitehead St at Mallory Square ■ 888-584-5927 ■ Open 9am–6pm daily ■ Adm ■ www.keywestaquarium.com

The Touch Tank here is a great attraction for children, allowing them to pick up starfish, native conchs, and horseshoe crabs. They even get the chance to pet a live shark. When it opened, in 1934, this was Key West's first tourist attraction, and it continues to draw crowds, not only for its hands-on features, but also for the highly entertaining and educational guided tours. Seeing the amazing and rare sawfish go to work during feeding time is a sight not to be missed.

Kids enjoying MeLab at the Phillip and Patricia Frost Museum of Science

6 Phillip and Patricia Frost Museum of Science

MAP G3 ▪ 1101 Biscayne Blvd
▪ 305-434-9600 ▪ Open 9:30am–
5:30pm daily; closed Thanksgiving
& Christmas ▪ Adm ▪ www.frost
science.org

The young and curious will find
much to capture their attention and
imagination here. There are over
140 hands-on exhibits to explore the
worlds of sound, light, and gravity,
not to mention the chance to hug a
dinosaur. Outside – beyond the collections of fossils, mounted insects,
spiders, and butterflies – lies the
Wildlife Center, home to birds, tortoises, and enormous snakes. The
state-of-the-art planetarium offers
laser light shows set to rock music.

7 HistoryMiami

The Downtown museum has
a number of hands-on activities and
multimedia programs, such as an
exploration of the Everglades' ecol-
ogy, past and present (see p42).

8 Cape Florida Lighthouse

Older kids love clambering
up this 95-ft- (30-m-) high lighthouse
(under-eights are not permitted to go
up), while the surrounding beaches
of Bill Baggs Cape Florida State Park
are fun for all the family (see p83).

9 Hobie Island Beach

An excellent stretch of beach,
popular not only with windsurfers
but also with families appreciative
of its calm, shallow waters (see p50).

10 Boat Tours Biscayne Bay

MAP P1 ▪ Island Queen
Cruises 402 Biscayne Blvd, Bayside
Marketplace ▪ 800-910-5118
▪ Every hour 11am–7pm daily
▪ www.islandqueencruises.com

Narrated boat tours are the best way
to see the islands of Biscayne Bay –
the tranquil stretch of water between
Downtown and Miami Beach – which
is dominated by opulent mansions
owned by celebrities such as
Shaquille O'Neal and Oprah Winfrey.

Boat sightseeing tour, Biscayne Bay

🔟 Performing Arts Venues

Entrance to the Colony Theatre

1 Colony Theatre
MAP Q2 ■ 1040 Lincoln Rd, South Beach ■ 800-211-1414 ■ www.colonytheatremiamibeach.com
This state-of-the-art venue presents some of the city's best classical music concerts, dance, theatrical performances, and experimental film.

2 Kravis Center
MAP D2 ■ 701 Okeechobee Blvd, West Palm Beach ■ 561-832-7469 ■ www.kravis.org
Home to the Miami City Ballet, Palm Beach Opera, and Palm Beach Pops, this performing arts center comprises a concert hall, the Rinker Playhouse, the smaller Helen K. Persson Hall and an outdoor amphitheatre.

3 Miracle Theatre
MAP G3 ■ 280 Miracle Mile, Coral Gables ■ 305-444-9293 ■ www.actorsplayhouse.org
The 1940s Deco-style movie theater was converted into a playhouse in 1995 and has won accolades for musicals such as *West Side Story*.

4 Olympia Theater
The Olympia Theater, located in Downtown Miami, is a major venue offering a varied program of plays, music, dance, and film *(see p95)*.

5 Adrienne Arsht Center for the Performing Arts
MAP G3 ■ 1300 Biscayne Blvd ■ 305-949-6722 ■ www.arshtcenter.org
This spectacular complex includes three state-of-the-art theaters, the Ziff Ballet Opera House, Knight Concert Hall, and a restored Art Deco Tower.

6 Broward Center
MAP D3 ■ 201 SW 5th Ave, Fort Lauderdale ■ 954-462-0222 ■ www.browardcenter.org
Major arts center in Fort Lauderdale, opened in 1991 at the heart of the Riverwalk Arts and Entertainment District. Key partners include the Symphony of the Americas, Florida Grand Opera, and Miami City Ballet.

Alexander W. Dreyfoos, Jr. Concert Hall, the largest venue at the Kravis Center

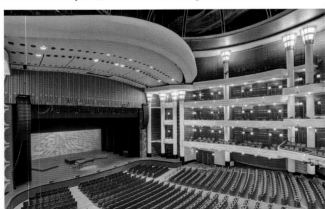

Wertheim Performing Arts Center

MAP F3 ▪ 10910 SW 17th St ▪ 305-348-0496 ▪ www.carta.fiu.edu/wpac

West of Downtown on the campus of Florida International University, this state-of-the-art venue comprises the Mainstage Theatre, the Concert Hall, and the Black Box Studio Theatre. It is also home to the FIU School of Music and Department of Theatre.

8 The Fillmore Miami Beach at the Jackie Gleason Theater

MAP R2 ▪ 1700 Washington Ave, South Beach ▪ 800-854-2196

Following a massive transformation in 2007, the Jackie Gleason Theater now hosts a variety of performances in its 2,600-seat facility.

New World Symphony concert

 New World Center

MAP R2 ▪ 500 17th St, South Beach ▪ 305-673-3331 ▪ www.new worldcenter.com

Home to the New World Symphony, which is made up of music college graduates. The young virtuosos perform gospel, Piazzolla tango, symphonies, and chamber works.

10 Miami-Dade County Auditorium

MAP G3 ▪ 2901 W Flagler St ▪ 305-547-5414

Built in 1951, this Deco-style venue is proud to have been one of the first in the country to host the late Luciano Pavarotti, when he was still a virtual unknown. Operas, concerts, and touring events all benefit from the excellent acoustics in the auditorium.

TOP 10 ENTERTAINERS

Cher, a former SoBe resident

1 Cher
You can see where the ageless diva lived with Sonny on the water in Fort Lauderdale and South Beach.

2 Don Johnson
The star of *Miami Vice*, this King of 1980s Cool helped put hip "new" South Beach on the map *(see p83)*.

3 Jackie Gleason
"The Great One," who practically invented early American television, brought his *Jackie Gleason Show* permanently to Miami in 1964.

4 Madonna
She had a palatial spread next to Vizcaya for a while, and still owns a piece of the Delano Hotel restaurant.

5 Dave Barry
The newspaper humorist and author has helped to create Miami's image as an over-the-top urban free-for-all.

6 Gloria Estefan
The symbol of unstoppable Cuban Power for many, this pop songstress has succeeded in building an impressive cultural and real-estate empire.

7 Rosie O'Donnell
The talkshow hostess calls Miami home and is involved in local politics.

8 Jennifer Lopez
This Latino actress and songstress has owned a mansion and estate at Miami Beach since 2002.

9 Ricky Martin
Another Latino superstar, Ricky Martin owns real estate here.

10 Tito Puente, Jr.
The talented musician and son of the famed Latin bandleader has made South Florida home, where he promotes gay causes.

🔟 LGBT+ Venues

1 Beach at 12th Street, SoBe

MAP S3–4

This beautiful sandy stretch of SoBe, with its rainbow flags flying, is one of the most popular beaches among the LGBT+ community.

Beach at Fort Lauderdale

2 Fort Lauderdale Gay Beaches

MAP D3

Two major beaches in the Fort Lauderdale area are LGBT+ friendly, and particularly popular with gay men: Sebastian Street Beach; and John U. Lloyd State Park Beach.

3 Haulover Park Beach, Miami Beach

MAP H1

Everyone is welcome at this pristine stretch of shoreline. The northern portion is a designated nude area where clothing is very much optional.

4 Pride Center at Equality Park

MAP D3 ▪ 2040 N Dixie Hwy, Wilton Manors ▪ 954-463-9005

Located in Wilton Manors (with its sizable LGBT+ population), this is a big and well-maintained center. There's an extensive library of gay literature and reference works, friendly and helpful staff, a full calendar of special events, and plenty of opportunities for lively social interaction.

5 Village Pub

MAP D3 ▪ 2283 Wilton Dr, Wilton Manors ▪ 754-200-5244 ▪ Open 11am–2am Sun–Thu, 11am–3am Fri & Sat ▪ www.villagepubwm.com

This is another Wilton Manors mainstay, beloved for its open-air patio, all-day two-for-one "happy hour," and dancing until 3am. Drag shows take place on Thursdays from 11pm, there are fun karaoke nights on Wednesdays, and even a gameshow hosted by drag queen Misty Eyez on Mondays.

Vendors and picnic tables on Wilton Drive, Wilton Manors

6 Shoppes of Wilton Manors, Broward County

MAP D3 ■ 2262 Wilton Drive

A few miles north of Fort Lauderdale, the small town of Wilton Manors has one of the highest percentages of gay residents in America. The progressive town houses various gay-friendly shops, restaurants, and services.

7 Georgie's Alibi

MAP D3 ■ 2266 Wilton Drive, Wilton Manors ■ 954-565-2526 ■ www. georgiesalibi.com

This restaurant, sports bar, and video bar opened in 1997 in what was a rundown area, but Wilton Manors has since blossomed and this bar has flourished with it. In fact, the Alibi is one of South Florida's best gay venues, churning out American classics, while nightly drink specials keep costs low for the wallet-weary.

8 Ramrod, Fort Lauderdale

MAP D3 ■ 1508 NE 4th Avenue ■ 954-763-8219

Fort Lauderdale's Ramrod is a great spot to enjoy a cold beer and to meet a lively crowd. The place is packed with revelers on Friday and Saturday nights. There's usually a line at the door, but it's worth the wait. Fantastic DJs make this a great party scene along with fetish competitions for the raunchier set.

Gay and Lesbian Community Center

9 Boardwalk, Fort Lauderdale

MAP D3 ■ 1721 North Andrews Ave ■ 954-463-6969

A huge nightclub that attracts big crowds, this is a vibrant place with dancers performing every night. Drag shows are put on at the weekends, and happy hour is 3–9pm.

10 Gay and Lesbian Community Center, Key West

The center offers a library, a lounge, and all the information you need. Pluses include a monthly calendar of special events, such as wine-and-cheese parties, discussion groups, and a film series. Free anonymous HIV testing is available, or just stop by for advice and a chat (see p129).

🔟 Nightlife

Dancing at Dream Nightclub

1 Dream Nightclub

Rub shoulders with the rich and famous at Dream. It is a paragon of SoBe nightlife catering to the likes of LeBron James, Kim Kardashian, and the entire cast of *The Jersey Shore*. The drinks are pricey, but the experience is worth it *(see p87)*.

2 SkyBar

A SoBe nightlife hotspot, this attracts both locals and tourists with its eclectic mix of music – from 1980s rock to contemporary beats. The action is non-stop, with DJs and featured guests on hand to entertain the crowds *(see p87)*.

Open to the stars, the glam SkyBar

3 Twist

SoBe's premier gay venue is enormous, hugely popular, and always jumping, but it doesn't get started until very late, of course, and then it goes till dawn. Don't show up before midnight unless you want to be considered a desperate wallflower *(see p86)*.

4 Salsa Mia
MAP S4 ■ 900 Ocean Drive ■ 305-458-4558

If you want an active outing, try the two-hour Salsa class and learn to sway to the sizzling sound of a live band performing Miami's signature music. Dance lessons and party packages are available until 5am.

5 Blume Nightclub
MAP N4 ■ 1421 S Miami Ave ■ 305-577-9811

A glamorous club and lounge bar with high-end bottle service, Blume is decorated with tropical, floral motifs and a huge LED chandelier. Catch your breath at the tranquil garden bar terrace.

6 Whisper Cocktail Lounge
MAP N3 ■ 485 Brickell Ave ■ 305-503-4417

This fashionable lounge bar and nightclub on the 50th floor of the

W Miami Hotel boasts spectacular views, Japanese woodblock-inspired prints, plants, a pool, DJs, and dancing till 5am every weekend.

7 Copa Room Show and Nightclub

A truly all-inclusive venue with a Latin flair, this Miami Beach former-theater space offers Las Vegas-type shows, nightclub acts, entertainers, and late-night dancing all rolled into one evening *(see p87)*.

Partyers on the beach, Nikki Beach

8 Nikki Beach Miami

This beachfront complex is a playground for the Euro-hip and trendy denizens of SoBe. Nikki Beach is located on the first floor and Club 01 is on the second. There are new themes and dances every week, fashion shows, and interactive entertainment *(see p87)*.

9 Cameo

Housed in an architectural gem, the former Cameo Theater, this is high-tech fun at its most cutting-edge. Cameo is glitzy and full of attitude, with a busy program of parties and clubnights. You should definitely dress to impress for the fancy VIP area *(see p87)*.

10 Mynt

Enjoy a menu of custom cocktails at this vibrant, hot nightspot in South Beach. The flashy crowd here, including the celebrity elite, enjoy partying in style to house and hip-hop tunes, although there is no real dance floor *(see p87)*.

TOP 10 TROPICAL TIPPLES

Mojito cocktail infused with mint

1 Mojito
Papa Hemingway's favorite splash: light rum, crushed mint leaves, sugar, and lime to taste. Sublime!

2 Hurricane
Mix dark and light rums, blue Curaçao, and lemon juice, and enjoy.

3 Piña Colada
The blend of coconut milk, pineapple juice, and rum is impossible to beat.

4 Rum Runner
Shades of Prohibition-era Caribbean smugglers, this classic comes in many styles and fruity flavors: watermelon, grenadine, blackberry, etc.

5 Sangria
The variations of fruit added to the red wine are almost endless.

6 Cosmopolitan
Variations on this vodka and Cointreau theme are creative. Often done with cranberry and/or orange notes.

7 Daiquiri
Another timeless Caribbean rum concoction, any way you like it: mango, strawberry, lime, peach, guava, etc.

8 Margarita
This south-of-the-border treat, in regular and frozen incarnations, may be paired with any fruit and a range of liqueurs, too.

9 Mai Tai
One version of this Polynesian perennial features crème de noyaux, banana, grenadine, and tropical juices.

10 Martini
Be prepared for this old standby to appear on the menu in a thousand creative guises: with unexpected fruit liqueurs, for example, or even blended with white or milk chocolate.

🔟 Restaurants

A traditional Haitian dining room at Tap Tap, South Beach

1 Tap Tap, South Beach

Colors and more colors greet the eye everywhere you look, most of it semi-religious imagery depicting various beneficent Voodoo gods and goddesses. Hearty, simple, and spicy Haitian flavors are what stimulate the palate at Tap Tap (see p89).

2 Michael's Genuine Food and Drink

Chef and owner Michael Schwartz provides passion on every plate at this award-winning neighborhood gem. Pizza from the wood-burning oven is especially good (see p103).

3 Caffe Abbracci, Coral Gables

Enjoy authentic Italian cuisine at this local favorite. The formal ambience is perfect for a special occasion. Try the lobster-filled ravioli or the gnocchi in an *amatriciana* (pork cheek and tomato) sauce (see p113).

4 Barton G – The Restaurant, Miami Beach

Exquisitely presented food can be enjoyed here in the pleasant orchid garden or the stylish bar. Barton G knows how to do relaxed elegance really well (see p89).

5 The Forge Restaurant and Winebar, Miami Beach

At this Miami institution you can rub elbows with the city's upper crust and celebrities as you devour exquisitely prepared steak and lamb dishes. With an impressive wine list and six dining rooms, each decorated in a different style, it is the place to see and be seen (see p89).

6 Joe's Stone Crab, South Beach

A South Beach institution that is always packed – you might need to book a table well in advance. Located right on the beach, it's consistently excellent, although considered a bit too touristy for some. Closed August to mid-October (see p89).

Jumbo claws at Joe's Stone Crab

CVI.CHE 105

Contemporary Peruvian restaurant helmed by Juan Chipoco. Best known for its exceptionally fresh and zesty ceviches, the restaurant occupies a chic space adorned with eclectic artwork (see p97).

Palme d'Or, Coral Gables

Found in the prestigious Biltmore Hotel, this award-winning restaurant takes French fine dining to an entirely new level. Expect the freshest seafood, locally sourced ingredients, and a near-perfect wine list (see p113).

Versailles, Little Havana

Everybody's favorite Cuban hub is a must-stop on a visit to Little Havana – this is a busy, rambunctious place. The restaurant offers authentic Cuban fare and a convivial atmosphere, and there is a bakery next-door too (see p97).

Versailles, thronging with customers

Le Bouchon du Grove, Coconut Grove

Loved by locals, this French bistro is always jam-packed at lunchtime. Colorful posters on the wall, freshly baked croissants, and delicious desserts make this cozy eatery one of the best places for a casual meal. Outside tables are at a premium for a view of the busy main street (see p113).

TOP 10 FLORIBBEAN FOOD AND DRINK

Blackened grouper

1 Blackened Grouper
Having your fish cooked "blackened" is a Cajun recipe that has caught on in most restaurants in South Florida.

2 Conch Chowder or Fritters
The snail- or slug-like creature that lives in beautiful pink shells is served up in a traditional, rather chewy dish.

3 Black Beans and Rice
"Moors and Christians" is the staple of the Cuban diet. Its savory, smoky flavor complements almost everything.

4 Yucca/Plantain Chips
The variations on bananas and potatoes are often served as deep-fried chips – slightly sweet and wonderfully aromatic.

5 Café Cubano (Cafecito)
A tiny cup of intensely sweet, black coffee; this is the mainstay of life for many. If you want it with a drop of milk, ask for a *cortadito*.

6 Cevíche
A seafood marinade using lime juice, onions, green bell peppers, and cilantro (coriander).

7 Lechon Asado
Pork is a big part of the Cuban diet. This term translates as "roast suckling pig," and is the ultimate feast.

8 Chimichurri
A sauce of olive oil, garlic, lemon juice or wine vinegar, and parsley. Jalapeño peppers are optional.

9 Key Lime Pie
The Key lime looks more like a lemon but makes the most exquisite pie.

10 Alfajores
A typical Cuban pastry composed of chocolate, custard, and coconut.

For a key to restaurant price ranges see p89

🔟 Chic Shopping Centers

2 Village of Merrick Park
MAP G3 ▪ Miracle Mile, Coral Gables ▪ www.villageofmerrick park.com

The Village of Merrick Park offers luxury retail stores amid a posh urban garden ideal for concerts. At its heart are Neiman Marcus and Miami's first Nordstrom, along with fine shops and restaurants, such as the elegant Palm Restaurant. The Mediterranean Revival style, with landscaped walkways and fountains, was pioneered by the city's founder George Merrick (see pp24–5).

3 Las Olas Boulevard and the Galleria
MAP D3 ▪ 2412 E Sunrise Blvd, Fort Lauderdale ▪ www.galleriamall-fl.com

Fort Lauderdale's high-end shopping is spread between its main street downtown and a mall just near the beach. Las Olas's 100-plus boutiques are unique, and are interspersed with some really good restaurants. The Galleria (East Sunrise Blvd at A1A) offers Neiman Marcus and Saks Fifth Avenue.

4 Worth Avenue, Palm Beach
Loads of marvelously expensive, ultra-exclusive must-haves for the rich and famous (see p30).

1 Bal Harbour Shops
MAP H2 ▪ 9700 Collins Ave ▪ 305-866-0311 ▪ www.balharbour shops.com

The ultimate in chi-chi, down to the English spelling of "Harbour" (see p99). Here are the likes of Dior, Hermès, Gucci, Armani, Bulgari, Tiffany, Versace, and Louis Vuitton, not to mention Chanel, Dolce & Gabbana, Prada, and Lalique, all housed in a luxury, upscale mall surrounded by tropical gardens.

High-end Bal Harbour Shops

Aventura Mall, illuminated at dusk

5 Aventura Mall

MAP H1 ▪ Biscayne Blvd &
196th St, Aventura ▪ 305-935-1110
▪ www.aventuramall.com

Department stores Bloomingdale's
and Nordstrom are the upscale
anchors at this mall that offers three
levels of retail space. Specialty stores
include Henri Bendel, Anthropologie,
and Michael Kors. Art installations,
some excellent restaurants and cafés,
an international food court, and a 24-
screen cineplex complete the picture.

6 Dadeland Mall

MAP F4 ▪ 7535 N Kendall Drive
▪ 305-665-6226 ▪ www.simon.com

Fear not! There is a Saks Fifth
Avenue even way down in South
Miami – plus some 170 high-end
specialty shops and several other
fine anchor stores, including the
state's largest Macy's. Unless you're
shopping on the cheap, ignore the
fact that there's also a JC Penney,
a Radio Shack, and a Best Buy. The
decor is pleasing, if a bit predictable,
with palm-tree pillars and ceilings
painted to resemble the sky.

7 Collins Avenue from 6th to 9th Street, SoBe

This area is great to stroll and shop.
There are boutique hotels, cigar
shops, and coffee shops interspersed
with lower-priced stores like Chicos
and Payless Shoes. A variety of price
ranges makes this area one for the
whole family to shop in (see p85).

8 The Falls

MAP F4 ▪ 8888 SW 136th St
▪ 305-255-4570 ▪ www.simon.com

Semi-open-air arcades with waterfalls
and tropical vegetation form the backdrop to over 100 shops. Mostly upscale,
they include Bloomingdale's, Macy's,
Banana Republic, Pottery Barn, and
the Discovery Channel Store for kids.
In addition, there are 12 movie
screens, and 13 restaurants and cafés.

9 Town Center at Boca Raton

MAP D3 ▪ Town Center 6000 W
Glades Rd ▪ 561-368-6000
▪ www.simon.com

Boca's premier mall has been expan-
ded, and has taken a quantum leap
into even greater luxury. Set amid
exotic foliage, skylights, hand-glazed
tiles, and sculptural accents, there's
also a fancy cuisine court. Venture
into downtown Boca and stroll
through Mizner Park, where you'll
find more chic shopping options.

Town Center at Boca Raton

10 Duval Street, Key West

MAP A6

Besides tacky T-shirt shops, Key
West's main drag is home to superb
emporiums of quality merchandise,
including: clothing at Stitches of Key
West (No. 533); shoes at Birkenstock
(No. 612); Gingerbread Square Gallery,
mixing artists and world-class glass
blowers (No. 1207); and Archeo
Ancient Art, specializing in African
art and Persian rugs (No. 1208).

🔟 Malls and Markets

1️⃣ Sawgrass Mills Mall
MAP D3 ■ **12801 W Sunrise Blvd, at Flamingo Rd** ■ **954-846-2300** ■ **www.simon.com**
This is one of the country's largest outlet and retail centers, which you'll learn as you drive its circumference trying to find the way in. This 8-acre (3-ha) mercantile behemoth comprises more than 300 discount outlets, from top-of-the-line goods to bargain basement rejects.

Bayside Marketplace in the evening

2️⃣ Bayside Marketplace
Chain boutiques abound in this sprawling marketplace, with the occasional trendy local shop adding spice. It holds a prime spot right on the waterfront *(see p92)*.

3️⃣ Lincoln Road Markets
MAP R2 ■ **Lincoln Rd, between Washington Ave and Alton Rd**
A lively pedestrian area, graced with attractive fountains and upscale restaurants and shops, this also offers various markets. On Sunday, there's one selling fruit and flowers, plus regional products, and specialties. Every other Sunday from October to May, there's also a collectors' market, and on the second Tuesday of the month "Arts on the Road" features all sorts of work.

4️⃣ Seybold Building
Located just off Flagler Street, where all sorts of cut-rate electronics can be haggled over, this building specializes in gems and jewelry, both wholesale and retail. Although this is mainly a place for jewelers to pick up stock, everyone can rummage the sparklers and invest in either loose gems or unique pieces of fine jewelry *(see p96)*.

5️⃣ Los Pinareños Fruteria
Little Havana's foremost fruit and veg market sells produce that can be difficult to find elsewhere, and you can get fresh juice, snacks, and flowers, too *(see p96)*.

6️⃣ The Swap Shop
MAP D3 ■ **3291 W Sunrise Blvd, between I-95 & Florida's Turnpike, Fort Lauderdale** ■ **www.floridaswapshop.com**
Eighty-eight acres (35 ha) of shopping at bargain prices, entertainment, and fun, the Swap Shop serves 12 million shoppers a year. This huge outdoor/indoor flea market features antiques, collectibles, clothing, plants, and a farmers' market. In total there are some 2,000 vendors. Inside, in addition to an international food court and a video arcade, there are also amusement rides. The complex claims to have the world's largest drive-in theater with 14 screens.

7 Dania Beach Historic Antiques District

MAP D3 ■ Federal Highway 1 north for two blocks from Dania Beach Blvd

Here is South Florida's largest concentration of antiques shops. More than 100 dealers offer an array of furniture, fine art, and jewelry, as well as glass, pottery, and china, and various other collectibles. Prices vary greatly, so shop around for bargains.

8 Opa-Locka/Hialeah Flea Market

MAP G2 ■ 12705 NW 47th Ave

Up to 1,200 dealers show up at Opa-Locka seven days a week from 6am to 6pm, hawking everything and anything you can think of to satisfy an orgy of acquisition. Weekends are the most atmospheric, when the number of dealers, browsers, and bargain-hunters swells.

9 Española Way Market

MAP R3 ■ 15th St, South Beach

On Saturday and Sunday, there's a small, rather esoteric market along Española Way, selling flowers, arts and crafts, and organic products. An array of vaguely hippie items also make an appearance, such as amulets, scented candles, stones, oriental bric-a-brac, and exotic clothing – all natural, of course. You can get your palm read, too, or decorated with henna if you prefer.

Ramblas walkway, Dolphin Mall

10 Dolphin Mall

MAP F3 ■ 11401 NW 12th St ■ 305-365-7446 ■ www.shopdolphin mall.com

More than 200 stores are crammed into one of Greater Miami's most popular middle-range malls. In part, this is an outlet for the heavy hitters including Saks Fifth Avenue, Brooks Brothers, and Giorgio's, but there is also a good range of boutiques as well as a 19-screen cineplex at the heart of it all, on the "Ramblas," where a selection of lively eateries are found.

Shoppers enjoying the weekend market on Española Way

TOP 10 Miami and the Keys for Free

Aerial view of the sands, South Beach

1 A Day on South Beach

With so much happening on land, it can be easy to neglect Miami's biggest free attraction – the beach itself, and those famous candy-colored lifeguard towers (see pp12–13).

2 Mallory Square Sunset Celebration, Key West

MAP A6 ▪ Mallory Square Dock, Key West ▪ Begins at sunset ▪ www.sunsetcelebration.org

Key West's Sunset Celebration started in the 1960s. Today these nightly gatherings feature arts and crafts, jugglers, fire-eaters, food carts, and cheap cocktails as a backdrop for the sinking of the sun.

3 Holocaust Memorial

Miami's moving tribute to the Holocaust depicts a giant bronze arm tattooed with an Auschwitz number reaching toward the sky. The black marble walls around the sculpture are inscribed with the names of the victims of Nazi atrocities (see p38).

4 Miami Circle

MAP N2 ▪ Brickell Ave, Downtown ▪ Open access

Just across the Brickell Avenue Bridge south of Downtown Miami, a small park preserves the ring of 24 holes known as the Miami Circle. The site was discovered by accident in 1998, and the prehistoric shell-tools found here were used to carbon-date the site to between 1,700 and 2,000 years old.

5 Tour the Wynwood Walls

MAP G3 ▪ 2520 NW 2nd Ave, between NW 25th and NW 26th Sts ▪ 305-531-4411 ▪ Open 10:30am–11:30pm Mon–Thu, 10:30am–midnight Fri & Sat, 10:30am–8pm Sun ▪ www.thewynwoodwalls.com

The Wynwood district (see p100) is crammed with art galleries and adorned with giant murals known as the Wynwood Walls. The main group lies on 2nd Avenue, just to the north of Downtown Miami.

Detail of a mural, Wynwood Walls

6 Freedom Tower

Built in 1925, this 225-ft (69-m) tower earned its current name by acting as a reception center for Cuban refugees from 1962 to 1974. Today it's owned by Miami-Dade College (MDC) and houses its Museum of Art + Design *(see p90)*.

7 Stroll Along Lincoln Road Mall

Pedestrianized Lincoln Road Mall is an upscale shopping strip lined with fashionable brand-name stores and alfresco cafés; Sunday afternoons are especially lively *(see p82)*.

Palm-tree-lined Lincoln Road Mall

8 Cubaocho Museum

This dynamic Cuban-American cultural center hosts exhibits of Cuban art and a roster of live events. Visitors can also relax at a traditional café and a bar serving mojitos *(see p93)*.

9 Oldest House Museum, Key West

MAP A6 ▪ 322 Duval St, Key West
▪ 305-294-9502 ▪ Open 10am–4pm Mon, Tue & Thu–Sat ▪ www.oirf.org

Built in 1829, this is the "oldest house" on Duval Street. The museum inside chronicles the history of Key West through family portraits, original furnishings, and historic ship models.

10 Observing Key Deer on Big Pine Key

MAP B6 ▪ 305-872-0774
▪ Visitor center open 9am–4pm Mon–Fri, 10am–3pm Sat & Sun
▪ www.fws.gov/nationalkeydeer

Big Pine Key is known for its herds of feral Key deer. The best time to spot them is at sunrise or sunset.

TOP 10 BUDGET TIPS

Yoga enthusiasts, Bayfront Park

1 Free Yoga
Free yoga classes are offered daily at Bayfront and Museum parks.

2 Dine early
Seek out dinner deals such as early-bird specials for patrons dining between 5pm and 6pm. Save on restaurant meals and drinks by opting for the set menus.

3 Monthly art walks
Visit Coral Gables and Wynwood when the free monthly art walks/ gallery nights take place.

4 Travel during off-peak season
To save money avoid traveling during the peak season. January to April is the most expensive time.

5 Go to the beach
Beaches are free and open to the public, even if parking is not.

6 Try street food
Little Havana's Latino and Cuban restaurants are much less expensive than South Beach.

7 Go Miami card
Buy a Go Miami card to enjoy discounts of up to 55 percent at around 28 major attractions *(www.smartdestinations.com)*.

8 Take the bus
On arrival in Miami, save by taking the Miami Beach Airport Express bus rather than a taxi.

9 Free museums
Try to visit museums on free days, such as the Jewish Museum (Saturday) and The Wolfsonion-FIU (Friday nights).

10 Hire a bike
Not only is cycling healthier than driving, but it's also one of the best ways to see the sights.

🔟 Festivals

1 Winter Party and White Party

MAP R4 ▪ Winter Party first 10 days in Mar; White Party late Nov

These renowned annual gay beach parties attract thousands of visitors from all over the United States. Pumped-up raves go on all night in the choicest South Beach venues.

2 South Beach Wine and Food Festival

MAP R4 ▪ February
▪ www.corporate.sobe
wff.org

This popular festival celebrates the talents of renowned wine producers and local and guest chefs.

3 Carnaval Miami

MAP K3 ▪ 8th St from 4th–27th aves ▪ Approx first 10 days of Mar

For the Cuban district, March is a time of dancing and singing in the streets to Latin jazz, pop, flamenco, and tango. It culminates on the second Sunday with a large party. Twenty-three blocks of Little Havana are closed off and performers line the way. A fireworks display brings a resounding finale to the festivities.

4 Coconut Grove Arts Festival

17–19 February

The Grove is one of the biggest arts festivals in the country, complete with all-day concerts, street food, and throngs of arts lovers (see p110).

Miami International Film Festival

5 Miami International Film Festival

Early Mar ▪ www.miamifilm
festival.com

Organized by the Film Society of Miami and Miami Dade College (MDC), with a special focus on Ibero-American films. Venues include the Olympia Theater, Coral Gables Art Cinema, and O Cinema Miami Beach.

Dressed in colorful costumes, people take to the streets for Carnaval Miami

6 Miami-Dade County Fair and Exposition

MAP E3 ■ Tamiami Park, Coral Way & SW 112th Ave, West Dade ■ Mar/Apr

This traditional American county fair is replete with rides, sideshows, cotton candy, candied apples, live performances, and exhibits relating to farm life and crafts.

7 International Mango Festival

MAP G4 ■ Fairchild Tropical Botanic Gardens ■ 2nd weekend of Jul

The luscious fruit is celebrated with gusto – enjoy a complete mango feast.

8 Hispanic Heritage Festival

MAP G3 ■ Throughout Miami-Dade County ■ Sep/Oct

This month-long Latino blast has street parties, food festivals, films, music and dance performances, and even an Hispanic beauty pageant.

Key West Fantasy Fest parade

9 Key West Fantasy Fest

20–29 Oct

For two weeks leading up to Halloween, Key West gives itself over to non-stop celebration. On the Saturday before the 31st, a parade, featuring floats and costumes, departs from Mallory Square and slowly winds down Duval. Many revelers go nude, except for a bit of body paint here and a feather or two there *(see p127)*.

10 King Mango Strut

■ Last Sunday in December

A Coconut Grove spoof on the Orange Bowl Parade *(see p110)*.

TOP 10 MULTICULTURAL ATTRACTIONS

Miccosukee Indian Village

1 Little Havana
A little slice of Cuba *(see pp18–19)*.

2 Little Managua
Nicaraguan shops abound in the zone (also called Sweetwater) just west of Calle Ocho.

3 Little Haiti
Come here to check out a quirky *botánica* or two *(see p99)*.

4 Billie Swamp Safari Wildlife Center
Big Cypress Seminole Indian Reservation. The Seminole didactic style is "laugh & learn" *(see p34)*.

5 Ah-Tah-Thi-Ki Seminole Indian Museum
Exhibits on camp life, ceremonies, and the Seminole economy *(see p34)*.

6 Miccosukee Indian Village
25 miles west of Florida Turnpike ■ Open 9am–5pm daily ■ Adm
See basket-weaving, palmetto doll-making, beadwork, dugout carving, and alligator wrestling.

7 Overtown Historic Village
The African-American neighborhood has restored historic buildings such as Dorsey House, 250 NW 9th St *(see p56)*.

8 Lyric Theater
Now a reborn venue for African-American cultural events *(see p56)*.

9 Liberty City
Site of deadly race riots in 1980, this African-American neighborhood, west of Little Haiti, has many interesting murals and graffiti-inspired art.

10 Little Tel Aviv
Arthur Godfrey Rd is home to a Jewish Learning Center and a community services center, alongside restaurants, bakeries and Kosher supermarkets.

⓾ Drives and Walks

The swampy Everglades

1 Everglades Trails

There are several roads for exploring the Everglades: I-75 or Alligator Alley; Highway 41 or the Tamiami Trail; or the less developed road (No. 9336) from Florida City. Off all of these roads, you'll find several opportunities for great excursions into the wild (see pp34–5).

2 SoBe Streetlife

Almost synonymous with the Art Deco District. All the action is concentrated in three areas: Ocean Drive and the parallel streets of Collins and Washington (where most of the clubs are located); the seductive Lincoln Road and the Española Way pedestrian malls (see pp12–13).

3 Calle Ocho

The main walking part of Little Havana lies along SW 8th Street, between about 11th and 17th avenues. But the interesting

MacArthur Causeway crossing the bay

spots are quite spread out several blocks around, and most of them are best found by driving, then exploring on foot (see pp18–19).

4 Coconut Grove

Always lively, usually with a young crowd, this area of town south of Downtown has a great buzz and is ideal for exploring on foot. As well as shops, outdoor eateries, and cafés, live bands often play in CocoWalk (see pp106–13).

5 Palm Beach

Begin your walk at Worth Avenue on the beach at Ocean Blvd. Walk west and check out as many of the fabulous shops as you dare. Continue on to Addison Mizner's pink palace, Casa de Leoni (No. 450), then take Lake Drive north to Royal Palm Way. Visit the Society of the Four Arts, then continue north to the Flagler Museum. Finally, go east along Royal Poinciana Way and south to The Breakers (see p30).

6 Miami Beach to Tip of Key Biscayne

MAP H3–H4

From South Beach, drive west on 5th Street, which becomes the MacArthur Causeway, I-395. Great views are to be had over the water and the islands, notably Star, Palm, and Hibiscus. Soon you'll be soaring over Downtown on the overpass that leads around to I-95, getting a bird's-eye view of the many skyscrapers. Just before I-95 ends, take the exit for Key Biscayne. Stop at the Rickenbacker Causeway tollbooth ($1.75). The high arching road takes you to deserted Virginia Key and then to quiet Key Biscayne.

7 Key West Old Town

The only sensible way to get around Key West is either on foot or by bike; there's so much detail to take in and, besides, parking is usually a problem here. A planned tour can be fine (see p127), but it's just as good to walk wherever inspiration leads (see pp32–3).

8 Art Deco District

With some 800 Tropical Deco wonders to behold, you can hardly miss it; just walk or bike along Ocean Drive, and Collins and Washington avenues between about 5th and 22nd streets (see pp14–17).

The Ocean Drive, Art Deco district

9 Miami to Key West
MAP D4–A6

There are great sights along this drive, like the giant lobster at the Rain Barrel. Stop to have a seafood meal on the water. Other attractions include parks and nature preserves, such as Bahia Honda State Park (see p121).

10 Routes North

If driving north from Miami, take the Gold Coast Highway A1A – it makes the time spent decidedly worthwhile, rewarding the traveler with both natural beauty and the elegant neighborhoods of the Gold and Treasure Coasts (see pp30–31).

TOP 10 ROADSIDE DINERS AND FOOD STOPS

Diners at Mrs. Mac's Kitchen

1 Mrs. Mac's Kitchen, Key Largo
MAP C5 ▪ 99336 Overseas Hwy
No-frills diner famed for its fresh seafood and homemade chili.

2 Ballyhoo's, Key Largo
MAP C5 ▪ 97860 Overseas Highway
Conch house from the 1930s that features a Friday-night fish fry.

3 Alabama Jack's
MAP D5 ▪ 58000 Card Sound Rd
Tasty conch fritters and live music since the 1950s, on Highway 905A.

4 Hungry Tarpon, Islamorada
MAP C5 ▪ 77522 Overseas Hwy
Scenic views and tuna tacos, cracked conch and Thai-style mahi fish fingers.

5 The Seven Mile Grill, Marathon
MAP B6 ▪ 1240 Overseas Hwy
Well-known for its delicious conch chowder, beer-steamed shrimp, and Key lime pie since 1954.

6 No Name Pub, Big Pine Key
MAP B6 ▪ 30813 N Watson Blvd
The oldest pub in the Keys serves spectacular thin-crust pizzas.

7 The Village Grill & Pump, Lauderdale-By-The Sea
MAP D3 ▪ 4404 El Mar Dr
Atmospheric place for seafood, steaks and cocktails on Highway A1A.

8 Old Key Lime House, Lantana
MAP D2 ▪ 300 E Ocean Ave
Sublime Key lime pie and seafood in a house dating from 1889.

9 Joanie's Blue Crab Café, Ochopee
An Everglades pit stop serving such delicacies as frogs' legs, gator pieces, and Indian fry bread (see p137).

10 Robert Is Here, Homestead
This celebrated fruit stand always draws a crowd for the smoothies and Key lime milkshakes (see p119).

Miami and the Keys Area by Area

An aerial view of Florida Keys, a series of tropical islands

TOP 10 Miami Beach and Key Biscayne

Nowhere else on earth seems to be so addicted to glamour as Miami Beach. All the traits of modern life are here, pushed to the limit: symbols of wealth and status are vaunted everywhere you look in this style-conscious part of the city.

Key Biscayne, the next big island to the south, provides a contrast to the dynamism of its neighbor; here you will find a tranquil and family-oriented atmosphere pervading parks, perfect beaches, and a scattering of museums.

Cape Florida Lighthouse on the headland

MIAMI BEACH AND KEY BISCAYNE

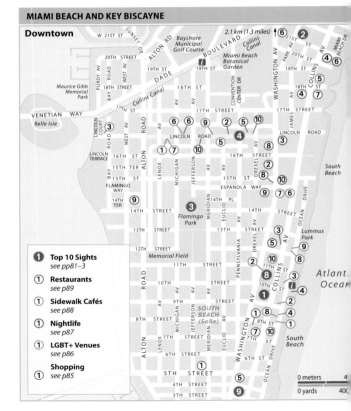

Downtown

Bayshore Municipal Golf Course

Miami Beach Botanical Garden

Maurice Gibb Memorial Park

VENETIAN WAY

Belle Isle

Flamingo Park

Memorial Field

SOUTH BEACH (SoBe)

South Beach

Lummus Park

Atlantic Ocean

South Beach

	Top 10 Sights see pp81–3
1	**Restaurants** see p89
1	**Sidewalk Cafés** see p88
1	**Nightlife** see p87
1	**LGBT+ Venues** see p86
	Shopping see p85

0 meters   4
0 yards   400

The world-famous Art Deco District, at the very heart of South Beach

1 SoBe and the Art Deco District

All walks of life meet here in the vibrant community of South Beach, otherwise known as SoBe

(see pp12–13). Its famous Art Deco District (see pp14–17) is beautifully preserved in hundreds of colorful, Tropical Deco buildings.

2 Bass Museum of Art

MAP S1 ■ 2121 Park Ave, South Beach ■ 305-673-7530 ■ Open 10am–5pm Wed–Sun ■ Adm ■ www.bass museum.org

This Mayan-influenced Art Deco structure of the 1930s, previously the Miami Beach Public Library and Art Center, came of age in 1964, when John and Johanna Bass donated their extensive collection of art. It consists mainly of 15th–17th-century European paintings, sculpture, and textiles; highlights include Renaissance and Baroque works, as well as paintings by Rubens, and a 16th-century Flemish tapestry.

3 Flamingo Park

MAP R3 ■ 11th Street and Jefferson Avenue, South Beach, Miami Beach ■ 305-673-7779 ■ Open Mon–Sun 8am–8:30pm

This pleasant spot in the heart of South Beach started life in the 1920s as a golf course. Later home to major and minor league baseball teams, the 36-acre- (14-ha-) park has since been extensively renovated. Today the site hosts an array of sports facilities, including baseball and football stadiums, basketball, handball, and tennis courts, and a soccer field. There is also an aquatic center with 2 public pools, and a playground for toddlers.

Miami Beach

1.6 km (1 mile)

See map left

Venetian Islands

VENETIAN WAY

MACARTHUR CAUSEWAY

Lummus Island

Biscayne Bay

Fisher Island

RICKENBACKER CAUSEWAY

Virginia Key

Biscayne Bay

CRANDON BOULEVARD

Key Biscayne

• Key Biscayne

Atlantic Ocean

km 1

miles 1

4 Lincoln Road Mall
MAP R2

Acclaimed as the most glamorous shopping district outside of New York when it debuted in the 1950s, this pedestrianized strip remains lined with hip brand-name stores and cool cafés. Russian-born "Miami Modern" (MiMo) architect Morris Lapidus designed the mall, including its gardens, fountains, and space-age follies that serve as sunshades. Attractions include ArtCenter/South Florida (at No. 924), where avant-garde artwork is displayed.

The unique facade of Lincoln Road Mall

5 Crandon Park
MAP H4 ▪ 305-361-6767

Key Biscayne is blessed with some of Miami's top beaches. Certainly the most impressive is this one, which is actually rated among the top ten in the country. Located on the upper half of the key, it's 3 miles (5 km) long and enormously wide, with palm trees and picnic areas. The waters are calm and shallow, and good for snorkeling. Additional bonuses include concession stands, 75 barbecue grills, a pretty winding boardwalk, and convenient parking.

6 Bill Baggs Cape Florida State Park
MAP H4 ▪ 305-361-5811 ▪ Adm

This beach, also rated among the nation's top ten, is conveniently joined to picnic areas and pavilions by boardwalks across the dunes. The sugary sand is sometimes marred by clumps of seaweed, but it is the stinging Portuguese man-o'-war that you need to watch out for most.

7 Marjory Stoneman Douglas Biscayne Nature Center
MAP H3 ▪ 4000 Crandon Blvd, Key Biscayne

Overlooking the ocean at the north end of Crandon Park, this center contains a unique black mangrove reef of fossilized wood and roots along the northeast shore of Key Biscayne. Wearing suitable foot protection, it is possible to wade in shallow waters to explore the underwater world. The nature center is named after the woman who almost single-handedly saved the Everglades from being overrun by housing developments, and it offers information and guided tours.

Beautiful Crandon Park Beach

Exterior of The Wolfsonian–FIU

(8) The Wolfsonian–FIU

A museum and design research institute that traces the origins of Deco and other significant modern artistic trends *(see pp28–9)*.

(9) Jewish Museum of Florida

MAP R5 ■ 301 Washington Ave, South Beach ■ 305-672-5044 ■ Open 10am–5pm Tue–Sun ■ www.jmof.fiu.edu

This fascinating museum chronicles the Jewish experience in Florida, with more than 100,000 items in the permanent collection. Highlights include a rare porcelain plate from 1865, an ornate ivory-covered Confirmation Bible printed in Vienna in 1911, and 19th-century community wedding rings from central Europe.

(10) Cape Florida Lighthouse

MAP H4 ■ Tours at 10am and 1pm Thu–Mon; 109 steps to the top

The oldest structure in South Florida has been standing sentinel since 1825. In 1836, it was destroyed by Native Americans, only to be reborn 10 years later. It has since withstood meteorological onslaughts, and in 1966 its renovation and preservation began.

MIAMI VICE

September 16, 1984, was a day that altered Miami overnight. It was the day *Miami Vice* debuted on TV, setting the stage for the city to conquer the world of high-profile glitz and hedonism. Suddenly the slick, candy-colored world of edgy outlaws, fast cars, and deals caught the global imagination, and Miami was the place to be.

A WALK THROUGH THE ART DECO DISTRICT

Abbey Hotel
Raleigh Miami Beach
Ritz Plaza
Delano
Collins Avenue
Loews Miami Beach
FL Café
Cardozo
Carlyle
Ocean Drive
Leslie
from 6th Street
1.6 km (1 mile)

▶ MORNING

From the southern end of the District on **Ocean Drive** *(see p13)*, at 6th Street, head northward, checking out not just the facades but also as many of the hotel interiors as you can. Many have unique design elements in the lobbies, bars, and gardens. Between the **Leslie** *(see p15)* and the **Cardozo** *(see p14)* is the wonderful Carlyle, now operating as a condominium. Turn left at 13th Street and walk to Collins Avenue. Turn right on Collins and stop for lunch at FL Café *(No. 1360 at 14th Street)*, set in an historic Art Deco building that dates to 1934.

AFTERNOON

A little farther on, you'll find the **Loews Miami Beach** *(see p148)*, which features a cut coral facade and neon lights. At No. 1685, admire the all-white **Delano** *(see p149)*, with its landmark winged tower. The outlandish Postmodern interiors are by Philippe Starck, and contain original Dali and Gaudi furniture. Next stop is the Ritz Plaza, with another fantasy glass tower block. When you get to 21st Street, turn left; on the next corner you will encounter the Abbey Hotel, with its marvelous salamander motif and Flash Gordon-style towers.

Cap the walk with a drink at the **Raleigh Miami Beach** *(see p150)*, a beautiful spot to end your day in the Art Deco District.

See map on pp80–81 ←

Sports Options

(1) Swimming

The hotel pool or the blue Atlantic Ocean? This is Florida, and swimming is number one – snorkeling, too, in quieter areas, especially Crandon Park on Key Biscayne (see p82) and South Pointe.

Windsurfers catching the wind

(2) Surfing and Windsurfing

For windsurfing in the area, the intracoastal waterways are calmer and there's always a breeze; check out Windsurfer Beach for rentals. The Atlantic side offers great conditions for surfing; the best spot is just off First Street Beach.

(3) Cycling

Miami Beach Bicycle Center: bikemiamibeach.com
Cycling is the best way to get around both Miami Beach and Key Biscayne.

(4) Jet-Skiing

Rentals are available at Hobie Island Beach and Jet Ski Beach at Virginia Key (see p50); weave through the waves and head for the horizon.

(5) Workouts

South Pointe Park has a "Vita Course," a fitness circuit you can huff and puff your way through while taking in the views of the port.

(6) Volleyball

Anywhere there's a developed beach you're likely to find a volleyball net and a quorum of players.

Lummus Park is the best place to show off your skills to Miami's greatest beach bums, but South Pointe Park's a close contender.

(7) Tennis

Miami-Dade County Parks and Recreation Department: www.miami dade.gov/parks ■ **Flamingo Park Tennis Center: www.miamibeach tennis.org**
There are plenty of tennis courts available for rental all over the area.

(8) Golf

Crandon Golf at Key Biscayne: MAP H4; 6700 Crandon Blvd; 305-361-9129; golfcrandon.com
The main reason that Jackie Gleason (see p61) moved to Miami is so that he could play golf year-round. The Crandon golf course on Key Biscayne is one of the best.

(9) Kite-Flying

This is a very popular activity, given the prevailing maritime winds. There's even a park especially for kite enthusiasts, which is located at the south end of Haulover Park.

(10) Fishing

Deep-sea fishing out in the ocean, or the more conventional kind off a jetty or pier – both are readily available. The jetty or Sunshine Pier at First Street Beach on Miami Beach is good, or the breaker area just south of the Lighthouse on Key Biscayne.

Anglers on the pier, Sunny Isles Beach

Shopping

1 **Collins Avenue from 6th to 9th Streets, South Beach**
MAP R4

This area has designer boutiques in ample supply from Armani Exchange and Aldo, to Kenneth Cole and Vidal Sassoon. Also present are mall favorites such as Guess, Nine West, MAC, and Banana Republic.

2 **Runway Swimwear**
MAP R2 ▪ 645 Lincoln Rd, Miami Beach

Look good on the beach with the latest swimwear fashions for men and women displayed at this store.

3 **Webster**
MAP S3 ▪ 1220 Collins Ave, Miami Beach ▪ 305-674-7899

Men's and women's fashions from top designers are available here. There's even a restaurant, Caviar Kaspia, where you can buy gourmet gift baskets to take home.

4 **Art Deco Welcome Center**

Besides a wealth of information about this historic district, you'll discover a treasure trove of Deco kitsch to take home as your very own. There's everything from cutesy salt and pepper sets to really rather nice reproduction lamps (see p15).

5 **Lids**
MAP R2 ▪ 521 Lincoln Rd, Miami Beach

With a large selection of sport apparel, fashion wear, and collegiate hats, Lids is the ideal place to purchase gifts that won't take up much room in your suitcase.

6 **Books and Books**
MAP R2 ▪ 927 Lincoln Rd, Miami Beach

Search the shelves for the perfect book to read while working on your tan. There is also a café serving good Pan-American food.

Gifts displayed at Babalu

7 **Babalu**
MAP Q2 ▪ 1111 Lincoln Rd, Miami Beach

This fashionable store has artfully curated designer clothing, home decor, fragrances, jewelry, and its own hand-crafted candy, which features flavors such as wild strawberry, juniper, absinth, peach, and rose.

8 **Fritz's Skate Bike & Surf**
MAP S2 ▪ 1620 Washington Ave, Miami Beach

Get yourself a pair of in-line skates, to rent or buy, and take some free lessons (Sunday mornings). Surf boards are available, too.

9 **The White Cotton Club**
MAP R3 ▪ 420 Espanola Way, Miami Beach ▪ 305-527-5399

Beat the Miami heat with clothes from this exclusive shop that features selections made with fine Egyptian cotton. The owners offer comfortable as well as fashionable apparel for both men and women.

10 **Goorin Bros Hat Shop**
MAP R2 ▪ 830 Lincoln Rd, Miami Beach

This is an outpost of the venerable hat makers established in Pittsburgh in 1895. Goorin Bros offers a made-to-fit service that considers face shape and head size, and there are a variety of styles from trilby, fedora, and top hat to cloche, caps, and knits.

See map on pp80–81

LGBT+ Venues

Diners eating outside at Balans

1 Balans
This London import is a firm favorite in the gay community. The global menu (including their signature lobster club sandwich) has a dash of British style *(see p88)*.

2 Twist
MAP R4 ■ 1057 Washington Ave, South Beach ■ 305-538-9478 ■ www.twistsobe.com
SoBe's largest gay venue, with seven bars in one, has something on every night. Happy hour 1–9pm daily.

3 Bar at Hotel Gaythering
MAP Q2 ■ 1409 Lincoln Rd, South Beach ■ 786-284-1176
A congenial lounge bar with a laid-back atmosphere, where soft ambient music does not overpower conversation. It specializes in micro beers and craft cocktails with names such as "Alexander Beaverhausen," while large HD TVs play hit shows and sporting events.

4 Big Pink Restaurant
MAP R5 ■ 157 Collins Ave, Miami Beach ■ 305-532-4700
This somewhat kitschy, retro diner-themed haunt is hard to miss thanks to the pink VW Beetles parked outside. The lengthy menu of comfort foods contains more than 200 items, and portions are huge.

5 The Cabaret South Beach
MAP S2 ■ Shelborne South Beach, 1801 Collins Ave, South Beach ■ 305-504-7500 ■ www.thecabaretsouthbeach.com
Popular piano bar and cabaret, serving up live shows Thursday to Sunday along with cocktails, bar snacks, and a full dinner menu.

6 Kill Your Idol
MAP S3 ■ 222 Española Way, South Beach ■ 305-672-1852
A statue of Bruce Lee hovers above the bar, and the Monday drag shows attract the biggest LGBT contingent.

7 Score
MAP S3 ■ 1437 Washington Ave, South Beach ■ 305-535-1111
SoBe's best mix of all-gay bar and dance club. It pairs a big-room interior with sidewalk-café style. Located right on Washington Avenue in the heart of South Beach.

8 Palace Bar and Grill
MAP S3 ■ 12th & Ocean, South Beach ■ 305-531-7234
The first gay restaurant/bar on Ocean Drive, in the heart of the Art Deco District. Popular for lively weekend drag shows, and varied menus.

9 Spris
MAP R2 ■ 731 Lincoln Rd, Miami Beach ■ 305-673-2020
Popular people-watching spot named after the famous aperitif from the Veneto. Eclectic menu of gourmet pizza and shareable plates.

10 Stiles Hotel
MAP S4 ■ 1120 Collins Ave, Miami Beach ■ 305-674-7800 ■ www.thestileshotel.com
Stylish boutique hotel and hangout located in the heart of the Art Deco District, popular with gay travelers.

VW Beetle, parked outside Big Pink

Nightlife

1 Club Space
MAP G3 ■ 34 NE 11th St, Miami
■ 305-495-8712 ■ www.clubspace.com
Known for its "all-night rage fests",
this club dares partygoers to stay
awake and watch the sunrise from
its terrace. House and techno DJs
play music all night.

2 Dream Nightclub
MAP S3 ■ 1532 Washington
Ave, South Beach ■ 305-674-8018
■ www.dreammia.com
An exclusive club popular with celebs,
this offers three themed nights:
"Fantasy Wednesdays," Latin, hip-hop
and reggaeton on "Enticing Fridays,"
and a hip-hop party on Saturdays.

3 MR JONES
MAP S2 ■ 320 Lincoln
Rd, Miami Beach ■ 305-602-
3117
Opening at 11pm, this club
stays lively until 5am. It
features hip-hop music.

4 Mynt
MAP S2 ■ 1921 Collins
Ave, Miami Beach ■ 305-532-
0727
Go – even if it's just to sample
a tipple or two from the
cocktail menu. This stylish,
sophisticated nightspot is
for a hip South Beach crowd.

5 Copa Room Show and Nightclub
MAP R3 ■ 1235 Washington Ave,
Miami Beach ■ 786-216-7785
■ www.coparoommiami.com
Originally built as a movie theater,
this Art Deco space hosts Las Vegas-
style shows with professional entertainers, singers, and even acrobats.

6 SkyBar
MAP S2 ■ Shore Club,1901
Collins Ave, Miami Beach ■ 305-695-
3100
This place offers four different areas
to choose from. Adventurous cocktails
are served, and an impressive array
of special guests entertain. Sunday
night draws the largest crowds.

7 Story
MAP R5 ■ 136 Collins Ave,
South Beach ■ 305-479-4426
■ www.storymiami.com
Huge club in an ornate, circus-style
setting, with a state-of-the-art sound
and light system and five bars.

8 Nikki Beach Miami
MAP R5 ■ 1 Ocean Drive, South
Beach ■ 305-538-1111
There are several bars and dance
floors here; downstairs is the upbeat
Nikki Beach, and upstairs the
exclusive Club 01.

Partying on the dance floor at LIV

9 LIV
MAP H3 ■ 4441 Collins Ave,
Miami Beach ■ 305-538-2000
The party crowd, including celebrities
and locals, frequent this massive,
high-energy, and exclusive dance
club located in the Fontainebleau
Miami Beach.

10 Cameo
MAP S3 ■ 1445 Washington
Ave, South Beach ■ 786-235-5800
Housed in the former Cameo movie
theater, the flashy interior and
futuristic lighting at this unique party
space give you the sense of floating
in a Surrealist's dreamworld.

See map on pp80–81

Sidewalk Cafés

1 News Café
MAP S4 ▪ 800 Ocean Drive,
at 8th St ▪ $

Open 24 hours on Ocean Drive,
this place is spacious and bustling.
Perfect for a drink, snack, or meal,
and avid people-watching *(see p12)*.

2 Mango's Tropical Café
MAP S4 ▪ 900 Ocean Drive,
at 9th St ▪ $

Always hot, with a huge Floribbean
menu. The action spills outside.

3 Clevelander
MAP S4 ▪ 1020 Ocean Drive,
South Beach ▪ $

Facing the beach on the sidewalk,
this always has something going
on: listen to the live music, have
something to eat, or just relax.

4 Pelican Café
MAP S4 ▪ 826 Ocean Drive,
South Beach ▪ $

Grab a seat on the outdoor patio and
indulge yourself, just as Cameron
Diaz, Antonio Banderas, and Johnny
Depp have before you, in partaking of
the Mediterranean-style delectables.

5 Nexxt Café
MAP R2 ▪ 700 Lincoln Rd,
South Beach ▪ 305-532-6643 ▪ $

In the heart of this popular shopping
street, Nexxt serves huge portions
from an extensive menu, at all hours.
Sit outside to people-watch.

6 Hofbräu Beer Hall Miami
MAP R2 ▪ 943 Lincoln Rd,
Miami Beach ▪ 305-538-8266 ▪ $$

From the legendary Hofbräuhaus in
Munich comes this authentic outpost
serving traditional German brews.

7 Balans
MAP R2 ▪ 1022 Lincoln Rd,
South Beach ▪ 305-534-9191 ▪ $$

An eclectic mix of Mediterranean and
Asian influences, this London-style café
is a popular SoBe standard-bearer.
Great for a non-buffet Sunday brunch.

8 Larios on the Beach
MAP S4 ▪ 820 Ocean Drive,
South Beach ▪ $

Co-owned by Cuban pop songstress
Gloria Estefan, this place prepares
cocina cubana SoBe-style. Try the
appetizer sampler and some *rico
mojitos* – a rum drink with mint leaves.

9 La Marea at the Tides
MAP S3 ▪ 1220 Ocean Drive,
South Beach ▪ $

Sit where celebrities have sat at this
chic outdoor café, and enjoy the glob-
ally inspired food and eclectic cocktails.

10 Wet Willie's
MAP S4 ▪ 760 Ocean Drive,
South Beach ▪ $$

This bar attracts a young, post-beach
crowd with its powerful frozen drinks
with names such as Call-A-Cab.
Nibbles to accompany the drinks
include fried calamari.

Customers eating alfresco, Nexxt Café

Restaurants

① Tap Tap
MAP R5 ■ 819 5th St, South Beach ■ 305-672-2898 ■ $

Real Haitian food, some of it fiery with red chilies. Try the grilled conch with manioc or the shrimp in coconut sauce, with mango sorbet for dessert.

Elaborate wall murals, Tap Tap

② Prime 112
MAP R5 ■ 112 Ocean Drive, Miami Beach ■ 305-532-8112 ■ $$$

The South Beach elite tuck into juicy steaks and excellent seafood served by waiters in butcher-stripe aprons.

③ Joe's Stone Crab
MAP R5 ■ 11 Washington Ave, South Beach ■ 305-673-0365 ■ $$

Expect gloriously sweet stone crabs and a notorious wait to get in. Also fish, pork, lamb, and steaks, and Miami's best Key lime pie.

Crab dish, Joe's Stone Crab

④ Cleo
MAP S2 ■ 1776 Collins Ave, South Beach ■ 305-534-2536 ■ $$$

Inside the Redbury Hotel, this chic place serves Mediterranean-inspired cuisine, from shareable mezes to big plates of roast lamb and couscous.

⑤ Fratelli la Bufala
MAP R5 ■ 437 Washington Ave, Miami Beach ■ 305-532-0700 ■ $

The best pizza in town is served at this South Beach Italian eatery, cooked in a wood-burning stove.

PRICE CATEGORIES

For a three-course meal for one with half a bottle of wine (or equivalent meal), taxes, and extra charges.

$ under $35 $$ $35–$70 $$$ over $70

⑥ The Forge Restaurant
MAP H3 ■ 4232 W 41st St, Miami Beach ■ 305-538-8533 ■ $$$

This modernized restaurant offers a 65-item American-fare menu. An eight-room wine cellar guards rare vintages and the bar offers a variety of wines.

⑦ Puerto Sagua Restaurant
MAP R4 ■ 700 Collins Ave, Miami Beach ■ 305-673-1115 ■ $

Authentic Cuban fare is what brings queues out the door here. Regulars swear by the *ropa vieja* and oxtail.

⑧ Pane & Vino
MAP S2 ■ 1450 Washington Ave, South Beach ■ 305-535-9027 ■ $

Cozy Italian restaurant from Sicilian chef GianPaolo Ferrera, featuring candlelit tables, elegant decor, and authentic dishes with homemade pasta. Be sure to try Paolo's celebrated Cannolo Siciliano for dessert.

⑨ Barton G – The Restaurant
MAP Q3 ■ 1427 West Ave, Miami Beach ■ 305-672-8881 ■ $$

The lush orchid garden is a great setting for a romantic meal under the stars. Popular with locals, the food is Neo-Classical American.

⑩ Yuca
MAP R2 ■ 501 Lincoln Rd, Miami Beach ■ 305-532-9822 ■ $$

The name Yuca stands for Young Urban Cuban-Americans. South Florida's original upscale Cuban restaurant has Nuevo Latino cuisine, trendy decor, and live entertainment.

See map on pp80–81

TOP 10 Downtown and Little Havana

For many visitors, this part of Miami is a foreign yet fascinating land. Here along the Miami River is where it all started in the late 1800s, but it took the arrival of Cuban exiles from the 1950s on for Miami to come into its own. On these bustling streets, you will see that the Cuban community still thrives in the south, and the Latino influence in Miami continues to grow.

1 Freedom Tower
MAP N1 ■ 600 Biscayne Blvd, Downtown ■ Open noon–5pm Tue–Sat ■ www.mdcmoad.org

Built in 1925 in the Mediterranean Revival style, this Downtown landmark was inspired by the 800-year-old bell tower of Seville Cathedral. Once home to the now-defunct *Miami Daily News*, and in the 1960s a reception center to process Cubans fleeing Castro, the building was restored in 1988 to create a Cuban museum. Today it holds the MDC Museum of Art + Design.

The iconic Freedom Tower

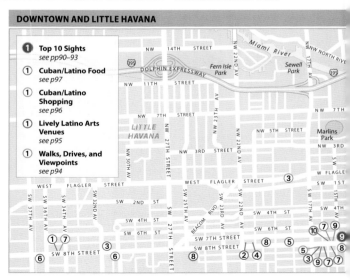

DOWNTOWN AND LITTLE HAVANA

- ① **Top 10 Sights** see pp90–93
- ① **Cuban/Latino Food** see p97
- ① **Cuban/Latino Shopping** see p96
- ① **Lively Latino Arts Venues** see p95
- ① **Walks, Drives, and Viewpoints** see p94

2 US Federal Courthouse
MAP N1 ▪ **301 North Miami Ave, Downtown** ▪ **Open 8am–5pm Mon–Fri, closed during major trials**

This imposing Neo-Classical edifice, finished in 1931, has hosted high-profile trials, including that of Manuel Noriega, the former Panamanian president, in 1990. The second-floor mural entitled *Law Guides Florida's Progress* is designed by Denman Fink, famous for his work in Coral Gables. It depicts Florida's evolution from a tropical backwater to one of America's most prosperous states.

Exhibit at Frost Museum of Science

3 Pérez Art Museum
MAP G3 ▪ **1103 Biscayne Blvd, Downtown** ▪ **305-375-3000** ▪ **Open 10am–6pm Mon, Tue & Fri–Sun, until 9pm Thu** ▪ **Adm** ▪ **www.pamm.org**

This premier art museum, set in lush gardens, showcases international and contemporary work. Designed by architects Herzog & de Meuron, its stylish galleries feature temporary exhibitions in a variety of mediums and a permanent collection including contemporary Cuban art donated to the museum by benefactor Jorge M. Pérez.

4 Phillip and Patricia Frost Museum of Science
MAP G3 ▪ **1101 Biscayne Blvd, Downtown** ▪ **Open 9:30am–5:30pm daily** ▪ **www.frostscience.org**

This museum relocated to new digs in 2017 (Miami entrepreneur Phillip Frost donated $35 million to the site). The campus features an aquarium, a planetarium, and the North and West Wings. The latter are crammed with interactive exhibits covering an exploration of the Everglades, the human body and mind, the story of flight, and the latest innovations in technology.

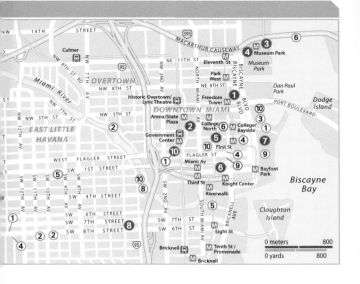

Bayside Marketplace running alongside the waterfront

5 Gesu Church
MAP N1 ■ 118 NE 2nd St, Downtown ■ 305-379-1424

This Mediterranean Revival building in the Spanish Colonial style (built in 1922) is the oldest Catholic church in Miami. The church is noted for its stained-glass windows and the ceiling mural restored by a lone Nicaraguan refugee in the late 1980s.

Detail inside the Gesu Church

6 Miami Tower
MAP N2 ■ International Place, 100 SE 1st St, Downtown

Built in 1983, this striking skyscraper is the work of architect I. M. Pei, famous for the glass pyramid in the courtyard of the Louvre in Paris. This building is notable both during the day for its Op-Art horizontal banding across the stepped hemi-cylinders, and at night for the changing colors of its overall illumination.

7 Bayside Marketplace and Bayfront Park
MAP P1–P2 ■ 401 Biscayne Blvd at 4th St, Downtown ■ Open 10am–10pm Mon–Thu, 10am–11pm Fri & Sat, 11am–9pm Sun ■ www.bayside marketplace.com

Curving around Miamarina, this shopping and entertainment complex is undeniably fun and the Downtown area's best attraction. It's not South Beach, but La Vida Loca echoes here, too, often with live salsa bands playing on the esplanade. Shops – including Guess, Victoria's Secret, Structure, and Foot Locker – and 30 eateries, with everything from ice cream to paella, make it a happening place. To the south, Bayfront Park, designed by Isamu Noguchi, is extensive and can provide a pleasant interlude of greenery, water, monuments, sculpture, and striking views.

GATEWAY TO LATIN AMERICA

Two-thirds of Miami's population is of Hispanic origin. Pick up the *Miami Herald* and you'll see that the news of the day in Caracas, Bogotá, Managua, and – above all – Havana is given top billing. All these connections, for good or ill, have made Miami the US kingpin when it comes to dealing with Latin and South America.

8 Calle Ocho and Around

This area is a slice of Cuban culture, liberally spiced up with all sorts of other Hispanic and Caribbean influences. Since Castro's Communist revolution in Cuba, Miami has become the main destination for wave after wave of immigrants fleeing the island that some still long for as home (see pp18–19).

9 Cubaocho Museum

MAP J3 ▪ 1465 SW 8th St, Little Havana ▪ 305-285-5880 ▪ Open 11am–8pm Sun & Mon, 11am–midnight Tue–Thu, 11am–3pm Fri & Sat ▪ www.cubaocho.com

The rich legacy of Cuban-Americans is celebrated at this cultural center established by collector Roberto Ramos, who escaped Cuba by boat in 1992. The main gallery displays a collection of pre-revolutionary art-work (1800 to the 1960s), including the massive 1937 painting "La Rumba" by Antonio Sánchez Araujo.

10 Miami-Dade Cultural Center

MAP M2 ▪ 101 W Flagler St, Downtown ▪ Library 10am– 6pm Mon–Sat

Designed by the celebrated American architect Philip Johnson in 1982, the Mediterranean-style complex, set around a tiled plaza, incorporates the informative, interactive HistoryMiami (see p42) and the Main Public Library, which contains four million books.

Miami-Dade Cultural Center

A TRIP THROUGH CALLE OCHO

▶ **MID-MORNING**

First stop, if you like a cigar, is the **Little Havana Cigar Factory** (see p19) on SW 11th Ave. Just across SW 15th Ave you will find the **Cubaocho Museum**. Soak up the exuberant collection of Cuban art here, perhaps grabbing a coffee at the café inside. Come back later that evening to catch live performances and enjoy an expertly made mojito at the bar. Next stop is SW 13th Avenue, to pay your respects to fallen Cuban freedom fighters at the **Brigade 2506 Memorial** Eternal Flame (see p18), before a sortie into the delightful fruit market at No. 1334, **Los Pinareños Fruteria** (see p96). At the corner of SW 15th Ave, peek in on **Dominos Park** (see p18) where there's always at least one game going on. Then take time to stop for coffee and maybe a snack at the wonderful **Exquisito** (see p97). Try to grab one of the vibrantly colored tables outside.

LATE MORNING

Continuing on to the next block, at No. 1652, take in the exciting Latin American art displayed at the **Agustín Gaínza Arts** gallery (see p96), where you're likely to meet the affable artist himself. After that, try a free-form ramble of discovery – but don't miss the gaudy entrance to **La Casa de los Trucos** (see p96), at No. 1343 – and when it's time for lunch, head for **La Carreta I** (see p97), on the south side of Calle Ocho. Enjoy good Cuban food at reasonable prices in this family restaurant.

See map on p90–91 ←

Walks, Drives, and Viewpoints

1 Bayside Marketplace
Adjacent to the impressive American Airlines Arena, this complex feels part Disney theme-park, part international bazaar. Located right on the waterfront, it's always good for a stroll (see p92).

Fun merchandise for sale, Calle Ocho

2 Calle Ocho Walk
Check out ethnic shops and sample various Cuban delicacies between 11th and 17th avenues (see pp18–19).

3 Flagler Street
MAP N2

Currently undergoing a $13 million renovation, walking through this area of Downtown Miami is reminiscent of a Latin American marketplace – colorful, brash, and rather seedy. Be wary at night.

4 Architectural Walk
MAP N1–N2

The buildings highlighted on pages 90–93 are lined up over about six blocks along NE–SE 1st and 2nd avenues. Another building worth a look is the Neo-Classical Revival Miami-Dade County Courthouse, three blocks away. Don't miss the ceiling mosaics in the lobby.

5 A Ride on the Metromover
The free Metromover consists of two elevated loops running around Downtown, so it's a great way to get an overview of the area (see p141).

6 Views of Downtown
MAP Q5 & M6

Some of the best views of Downtown are afforded from the freeways. Coming across MacArthur Causeway from South Beach, you'll get some dazzling perspectives, especially at night. The finest view of the skyline is from the Rickenbacker Causeway.

7 A Calle Ocho Café
The Exquisito Cafetería (see p97) is a wonderful place to listen to music and watch the fascinating street life all around.

8 A Stroll in José Martí Park
MAP M2

This charming little park by the Miami River is graced with colonnades and pavilions, Spanish-style clusters of street lamps, palm trees, and an excellent children's playground.

9 A Stroll in Bayfront Park
MAP P1–P2

Right on beautiful Biscayne Bay, this park was designed by Noguchi "as a wedge of art in the heart of the New World." Here, in addition to Noguchi's sculptures you will find lush greenery, a small sand beach, tropical rock garden, cascading fountain, palms, and olive trees.

10 A Drive Through Little Havana
To get the overall feel and extent of Little Havana, it's best to drive from José Martí Park in the west to about 34th Avenue in the east, where the Woodlawn Cemetery and Versailles Restaurant are (see pp18–19).

Cubaocho Museum, Little Havana

Lively Latino Arts Venues

The intriguing east facade of the Pérez Art Museum Miami

1 Pérez Art Museum Miami

This museum has a permanent collection of Cuban art. Wisredo Lamb, a modern Cuban artist, is represented in this section along with other Cuban artists *(see p91)*.

2 Teatro de Bellas Artes

MAP G3 ■ 2173 SW 8th St ■ 305-325-0515

This Calle Ocho venue presents eight Spanish plays and musicals a year. Mostly Spanish originals, there are also translations like Tennessee Williams' *A Streetcar Named Desire*.

3 Agustín Gaínza Arts

MAP J3 ■ 1652 SW 8th St ■ 305-644-5855 ■ www.agustingainza.com

A showcase for the work of Cuban-born Agustín Gaínza, whose *oeuvre* covers every medium from painting and printmaking to ceramics and even recycled bottles.

4 Teatro 8

MAP G3 ■ 2101 SW 8th St

Home to the Hispanic Theater Guild. Its directors try to choose topical plays that will become a force for renewal in the Cuban community.

5 Manuel Artime Theater

MAP L2 ■ 900 SW First St ■ 305-575-5057

A former Baptist church, this facility has been converted into an 800-seat state-of-the-art theater and is the home of the Miami Hispanic Ballet.

6 MDC Live Arts

MAP N1 ■ Miami-Dade Community College, Wolfson Campus 300 NE 2nd Ave, at NE 3rd St

The Performance Series presents music, dance, film, and visual arts, with an emphasis on contemporary works and solo theater performers.

7 Casa Panza

Great flamenco performances several nights a week at this authentic Spanish restaurant right in the Cuban heart of Calle Ocho *(see p97)*.

8 Casa Juancho

MAP G3 ■ 2436 SW 8th Ave ■ 305-642-2452

This popular restaurant in Little Havana serves up award-winning cuisine, as well as excellent Spanish performances, a piano bar, strolling guitarists, and a fine flamenco show.

9 Olympia Theater

MAP N2 ■ 174 E Flagler St

This major Downtown venue often features Latin American perform-ances of all types, including films during the annual Miami Film Festival.

10 Los Ranchos Steakhouse

MAP P1 ■ 401 Biscayne Blvd ■ 305-375-0666

Located in Bayside marketplace, this casual restaurant features Latin food and American steakhouse fare, plus regular Latin entertainment.

See map on pp90–91

Cuban/Latino Shopping

1 La Casa de los Trucos
MAP K3 ▪ 1343 SW 8th St
▪ 305-858-5029

This is the place to come for all your costuming needs. From the most predictable to the most bizarre, this shop has a vast inventory to buy or rent, and excellent prices.

2 Botánica El Aguila Vidente

This is the most atmospheric and mysterious of the *botánicas* along the main section of Calle Ocho *(see p19)*.

3 Havana Shirt
MAP P1 ▪ 401 Biscayne Blvd
▪ 305-373-7720

Get the best in Cuban shirts, as well as touristy beach shirts, from this store, which has a huge range. It is located in the trendy Bayside Marketplace shopping center.

4 Los Pinareños Fruteria
MAP K3 ▪ 1334 SW 8th St

A delightful fruit market with all sorts of exotic Caribbean produce, such as mamey and small "apple" bananas. There's also a fresh juice bar.

5 Agustín Gaínza Arts

The gallery is named after the celebrated Cuban artist whose work is on display here along with that of other contemporary Cuban and Latin American artists *(see p95)*.

Latino dolls for sale at Sentir Cubano

6 Sentir Cubano
MAP G3 ▪ 3100 SW 8th St
▪ 305-644-8870

Look for the vivid murals painted on the side of the building and you'll know you've arrived at this crazy store loaded with Cuban memorabilia.

7 Versailles Bakery
MAP G3 ▪ 3555 SW 8th St
▪ 305-441-2500

Delicious homemade pastries will satisfy your sweet tooth, plus desserts like flan and cheesecake accompanied by Cuban coffee.

8 Little Havana To Go
MAP J3 ▪ 1442 SW 8th St
▪ 305-857-9720

If you are interested in Cuban memorabilia, this store is bound to have it. Items on sale include reproductions of Cuban artwork, telephone books, and cigars.

9 Little Havana Cigar Factory

Enjoy the finest cigars money can buy. Expert staff are happy to make personalized recommendations *(see p19)*.

10 Seybold Building
MAP N2 ▪ 36 NE 1st St
▪ 305-374-7922

This building has several floors of jewelry and watches as well as wholesale and retail stores. The prices are good value and with so many choices, you will have a hard time deciding what to buy.

Artwork at Agustín Gaínza Arts

Cuban/Latino Food

PRICE CATEGORIES
For a three-course meal for one with half a bottle of wine (or equivalent meal), taxes, and extra charges.

$ under $35 $$ $35–$70 $$$ over $70

1 Versailles Restaurant
MAP G3 ▪ 3555 SW 8th St, at SW 35th Ave ▪ 305-444-0240 ▪ $$
A Little Havana institution, Versailles is actually a Cuban diner in a very sleek guise (see p67).

2 Garcia's Seafood Grille & Fish Market
MAP L1 ▪ 398 NW North River Dr ▪ 305-375-0765 ▪ $
A family-run eatery with a friendly atmosphere, though you might have a bit of a wait. Great grouper chowder and conch salad.

3 El Atlakat
MAP G3 ▪ 3199 SW 8th St ▪ 305-649-8000 ▪ $$
The cuisine of El Salvador, served in a spacious, cheerful setting. Pleasant murals, and a menu that leans toward chicken and seafood.

4 CVI.CHE 105
MAP P1 ▪ 105 NE 3rd Ave ▪ 305-577-3454 ▪ $$
Chic Peruvian restaurant displaying eclectic artwork, and helmed by Juan Chipoco, who is well-known for his tasty, fresh, and zesty ceviches.

5 El Rey De Las Fritas
MAP J3 ▪ 1821 SW 8th St ▪ 305-644-6054 ▪ $
No-frills Cuban diner specializing in Cuban-style burgers (ground beef patty topped with sautéed onions, thinly sliced fried potatoes and a special sauce), known as *fritas*.

6 La Carreta
MAP G3 ▪ 3632 SW 8th St ▪ 305-444-7501 ▪ $
From the food to the clientele, this family restaurant in the heart of Little Havana is thoroughly Cuban. Good food at reasonable prices ensures its popularity. Open late.

7 Exquisito Restaurant
MAP J3 ▪ 1510 SW 8th St ▪ 305-643-0227 ▪ $
The most authentic and affordable on the street, where locals go every day. Gritty Cuban fare, like brain fritters and horse beef stew, goes down well with the "gringos."

8 Guayacan
MAP J3 ▪ 1933 SW 8th St ▪ 305-649-2015 ▪ $$
Cozy and unpretentious, this is Cuban fare with a Nicaraguan twist. Try the *pescado a la Tipitapa*, a whole red snapper deep-fried and drenched in a sauce of onions and peppers.

Spanish ambience at Casa Panza

9 Casa Panza
MAP J3 ▪ 1620 SW 8th St ▪ 305-644-3444 ▪ $$
A picturesque Spanish restaurant, known for its fine paella and authentic flamenco show. Rooms are cozy, with performers putting on a flamenco show several nights of the week.

10 El Cristo
MAP J3 ▪ 1543 SW 8th ▪ 305-643-9992 ▪ $
This old-fashioned restaurant set in the heart of Little Havana serves up classic Cuban dishes such as *ropa vieja* and *arroz con pollo*.

See map on pp90–91

🔟 North of Downtown

The areas north of Miami Beach and Downtown are an irreconcilable juxtaposition of urban sprawl and urban chic, with acutely deprived areas right alongside the playground of a wealthy elite. Although the beaches are among the city's greatest (and quietest), little else in the area is well known, and it receives few visitors. Nevertheless, there is local color to be discovered here. Some of Greater Miami's most fascinating historic sights, including one of the oldest buildings in the Americas, a thriving arts scene, and a range of fine dining options are all well worth seeking out.

Mural by Serge Toussaint in Little Haiti

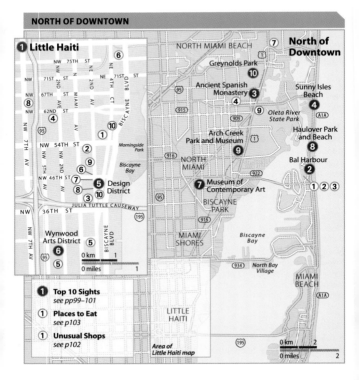

① **Top 10 Sights**
see pp99–101

① **Places to Eat**
see p103

① **Unusual Shops**
see p102

1 Little Haiti
**MAP G2 ■ NE 2nd Ave,
from about NE 55th to NE 80th
■ Marketplace at 5927 NE 2nd Ave**
Little Haiti can feel disconcerting to visitors – its contrast with wealthy Downtown Miami is striking. In 2006 the Little Haiti Cultural Complex was introduced here, aimed at promoting tourism and Afro-Caribbean culture. This vibrant center hosts arts events and concerts, and holds a Saturday market at its main venue, the Caribbean Marketplace.

2 Bal Harbour
MAP H2
The Barrier islands north of Miami Beach are occupied mainly by luxury residential areas, and this is the poshest. Known for its flashy hotels and one of the swankiest malls anywhere, Bal Harbour is said to have more millionaires per capita than any other city in the US. On Collins Avenue, Bal Harbour Shops is particularly fancy. Elsewhere along 96th Street are galleries, gourmet shops, and many plastic surgery studios.

3 Ancient Spanish Monastery
MAP H1 ■ 16711 W Dixie Hwy, North Miami Beach ■ 305-945-1461 ■ Open 10am–4:30pm Mon–Sat, 11am–5pm Sun ■ Adm ■ www. spanishmonastery.com
This monastery is the oldest European-tradition building in the Western Hemisphere, originally built in 1133–41 near Segovia, Spain. In 1925, William Randolph Hearst

Ancient Spanish Monastery

bought the magnificent cloisters, had them dismantled stone by stone, and sent to the US, where the stones were reassembled in the early 1950s for $1.5 million. Call before visiting on weekends as the monastery will close for events such as weddings.

4 Sunny Isles Beach
MAP H1 ■ Hwy A1A (north of Haulover Park)
The resort of Sunny Isles Beach is lined with high-rise hotels and condos, built to take advantage of the gorgeous beachfront. Landmark buildings include the residential Porsche Design Tower and its unique robotic parking garage. The area has a large expat Russian community, with caviar shops and Russian delis, restaurants, beauty salons, and real estate companies underscoring the area's nickname "Little Moscow."

Aerial view over Sunny Isles Beach

5 Design District

MAP G2 ■ Nr Buena Vista between NE 36th–41st sts and from NE 2nd to N Miami aves

It started out as a pineapple grove, but from the 1920s this zone was being called Decorators' Row because of the design stores that had moved in. For a while in the 1980s, due to high crime, the area fell on hard times, but things are picking up again, and top-end design, furniture, and fixture shops once again rule. Photographers and artists have been moving here, too, to escape the high rents of South Beach.

Design District luxury furniture store

6 Wynwood Arts District

MAP G3 ■ Bounded by N 36th St, N 20th St, I-95, and NW 1st Ave ■ www.wynwoodmiami.com

The former industrial warehouse district of Wynwood has been transformed into a vibrant neighborhood of art galleries, museums, clubs, and studios. Since 2009, huge murals – dubbed the Wynwood Walls (see p72) – have been a major element of the district's appeal.

CLASS AND CULTURE CLASH

Greater Miami is a bubbling cauldron of cultural diversity. Many endemically underprivileged African-American communities lie within a stone's throw of exclusive shops. In other areas, impoverished immigrants – recent arrivals from Cuba, Haiti, and other Central American countries – endure substandard living conditions in quarters of endless urban blight.

7 Museum of Contemporary Art

MAP G2 ■ 770 NE 125th St ■ 305-893-6211 ■ Open 11am–5pm Tue–Fri, 1–9pm Sat, 11am–5pm Sun ■ Tours on Sat at 2pm ■ Adm ■ www. mocanomi.org

The Museum of Contemporary Art opened its state-of-the-art building in 1996. It's known for its provocative exhibitions and for seeking a fresh approach in examining the art of our time. The permanent collection features emerging and established artists from the US and abroad.

8 Haulover Park and Beach

MAP H1 ■ 10800 Collins Ave ■ 305-947-3525

Haulover Park contains one of south Florida's most beautiful beaches – a mile and a half of golden sand drawing people from all walks of life. Nestled between the Intercoastal Waterway and the Atlantic, the beach is ideal for surfing and swimming, and on warm weekends it is jam-packed with sunbathers. The park itself has a marina, restaurant, tennis courts, a nine-hole golf course, and a kite shop. It is one of the nation's top ten nude beaches.

9 Arch Creek Park and Museum

MAP G2 ▪ 1855 NE 135 St

Created around a natural limestone bridge formation, this location used to be part of an important Native American trail. A museum/nature center contains artifacts left by those peoples. Naturalists will be your guides as they point out native birds, animals, insects, and trees.

Relaxing on the lawn, Greynolds Park

10 Greynolds Park

MAP H1 ▪ 17530 W Dixie Hwy

An oak-shaded haven for runners, golfers, and other outdoor enthu-siasts, Greynolds Park is landscaped with native and exotic plants, which include mangrove, royal palm, sea grape, palmetto, pampas grass, and gumbo limbo. You'll also find beach volleyball courts, a kid's playground, and plenty of picnic tables.

Wynwood Walls mural by artist, Case

A TOUR OF THE ANCIENT SPANISH MONASTERY

 MORNING

Drive north from central Miami on Highway 1 (also known as Biscayne Boulevard). The road is lined with shops – stop off at any that catch your eye. Turn left on NE 163rd St, then right onto W Dixie Highway (also NE 22nd Avenue). The **Ancient Spanish Monastery** *(see p99)* is on the right after the canal. You may well feel a sense of awe as you walk around this beautiful little piece of medieval Europe on US soil. Even European visitors, who will have visited many such buildings in their homeland, marvel at the dedication of Hearst to put it here. For the best route through the grounds, start at the gift shop/museum, exit to the patio, then through the gardens, cloisters, and interior rooms, culminating at the chapel. Among the notable sights along the route are a 12th-century birdbath, a life-size statue of the Spanish king Alphonso VII (the monastery was constructed to commemorate one of his victories over the Moors), and two of only three known surviving round stained-glass windows, also from the 12th century.

AFTERNOON

In keeping with the Spanish theme, eat at nearby **Paquito's Mexican Restaurant** *(see p103)* and take a detour along NE 2nd Avenue through colorful **Little Haiti** *(see p99)* on your way back.

See map on p98

Unusual Shops

Upmarket shops at Bal Harbour

natural and carved semi-precious gemstones, insects, shells, butterflies, skulls, animal mounts, and more.

6 Rebel
MAP G2 ■ 6669 Biscayne Blvd ■ 305-793-4204
Shoppers are bound to find something they want at Rebel, a high-end boutique that carries everything from everyday fashion to evening dresses.

1 Intermix
MAP H2 ■ Bal Harbour Shops, 9700 Collins Ave ■ 305-993-1232
Outfits for the discerning woman, whether 18 or 50. A great range of prices, labels, and accessories.

7 The Art of Shaving
MAP H1 ■ Aventura Mall, 19501 Biscayne Blvd, Suite 1527
As the name would suggest, this has a complete range of men's grooming products, and you can also get a haircut while you're there.

2 Addict
MAP H2 ■ Bal Harbour Shops, 9700 Collins Ave ■ 305-864-1099
Fashion sneakers for all the family, including rare sneakers not widely available in department stores.

8 Rasool's Menswear
MAP G2 ■ 6301 NW 7th Ave, #B ■ 305-759-1250
Famous for its alligator shoes for men, the store also stocks urban wear, dress suits, and T-shirts with creative artwork on them.

3 Oxygene
MAP H2 ■ Bal Harbour Shops, 9700 Collins Ave ■ 305-864-0202
The store has a wide selection of brand-name clothes, such as Armani, for women and children.

9 Bagua
MAP G2 ■ 4736 NE 2nd Ave ■ 305-757-9857
At this cool little store, with its fashion, home decor, spiritual gifts, and funky finds, it's all about feng shui, Buddha and everything Zen.

4 New Age Thrift Store
MAP H1 ■ 1734 NE 163rd St, North Miami Beach ■ 786-390-5866
This family-owned thrift store carries antiques, clothing, jewelry, and serviceable furniture at bargain prices. Look out for hidden gems such as quirky vintage and second-hand designer items.

5 Art By God
MAP G3 ■ 60 NE 27th St
Impressive mineral/nature store, with dinosaur fossils,

10 Jalan Jalan
MAP G2 ■ 3921 NE 2nd Ave ■ 305-572-9998
The owners constantly change this home design showroom to add global artisan pieces made of petrified wood, Belgian glass, and Indian marble work.

Pots from Jalan Jalan

Places to Eat

PRICE CATEGORIES
For a three-course meal for one with half
a bottle of wine (or equivalent meal),
taxes, and extra charges.

$ under $35   **$$** $35–$70   **$$$** over $70

1 Soyka
MAP G2 ■ 5556 NE 4th Ct
■ 305-759-3117 ■ $$

Run by the same fellow as the News
Café *(see p88)*, this is a huge, bistro-
like setting with an adventurous
Italianesque fusion menu. Try the
delicious sesame-seared salmon
with spinach and sweet soy sauce.

2 Chez Le Bebe
MAP G2 ■ 114 NE 54th St
■ 305-751-7639 ■ $

A Little Haiti no-frills establishment
with authentic Haitian food, from
tender *griot* (fried pork) to stewed
goat; all plates come with rice,
beans, plantains, and salad.

3 Michael's Genuine Food and Drink
MAP G2 ■ 130 NE 40th St ■ 305-
573-5550 ■ $$

The best restaurant in Miami's
Design District has a unique menu,
serving a range of fresh seafood
dishes, woodfired pizzas and
tempting brunch cocktails.

4 Clive's Cafe
MAP G2 ■ 5890 NW 2nd Ave
■ 305-757-6512 ■ $

A popular and good-value Jamaican
restaurant in the heart of Little Haiti,
serving delicious classics such as
jerk chicken and curry goat, as
well as salt fish for breakfast.

5 Panther Coffee
MAP G3 ■ 2390 NW 2nd Ave
■ 305-677-3952 ■ $

Miami's wildly popular small-batch
coffee roaster operates this café
in the Wynwood Arts District, with
local art on the walls and a menu
of cakes, cookies, and savory snacks.

6 Lemon Café
MAP G2 ■ 4600 NE 2nd Ave
■ 305-571-5080 ■ $

Cozy Design District café serving
wholesome food with a Mediterranean
slant, which is influenced by the
chef's French/Moroccan background.

7 Buena Vista Deli
MAP G2 ■ 4590 NE 2nd Ave
■ 305-576-3945 ■ $

Charming café in the Design District
serving homemade pastries and
coffee for breakfast, gourmet
sandwiches on artisan-crafted breads
for lunch, and lighter fare for dinner.

Pretty patio, Mandolin Aegean Bistro

8 Mandolin Aegean Bistro
MAP G2 ■ 4312 NE 2nd Ave
■ 305-576-6066 ■ $$

This stylish Design District eatery
recreates simple, rustic dishes
authentic to Greece and Turkey.

9 Paquito's Mexican Restaurant
MAP G1 ■ 16265 Biscayne Blvd
■ 305-947-5027 ■ $

Expect fresh tortilla soup, steak
Paquitos sautéed in a jalapeño and
onion sauce, and a yummy *mole verde*.

10 Andiamo!
MAP G2 ■ 5600 Biscayne Blvd
■ 305-762-5751 ■ $

Mouthwatering, brick-oven pizza pies
with a dizzying variety of toppings,
many of which are gourmet, can be
enjoyed here.

See map on p98

TOP 10 Coral Gables and Coconut Grove

Together Coral Gables and Coconut Grove constitute one of the most upscale neighborhoods in Greater Miami. The former was built by the real-estate developer George Merrick, who envisioned one of the first and most successfully planned suburbs in the US. Known as the "City Beautiful," it earns its moniker from winding avenues lined with elegant villas. Luxurious mansions and sailboats anchored in Biscayne Bay typify affluent Coconut Grove, where dining at a sidewalk cafe is a quintessential experience. The area has been constantly evolving since its bohemian days of the 1960s, and today its lively street scene makes it one of Miami's most vibrant districts.

Decorative lamp stand, Vizcaya Museum and Gardens

CORAL GABLES AND COCONUT GROVE

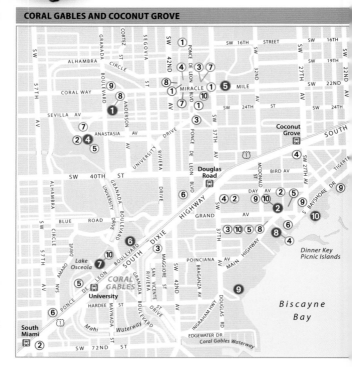

Dinner Key Picnic Islands

Biscayne Bay

Previous pages The Coguer, Coral Castle Museum

Merrick's beautiful Venetian Pool

1 Venetian Pool
MAP G3

This is one of the loveliest and most evocative of Merrick's additions to his exotic vision for Coral Gables. The pool is fed by springs and was the site of at least one movie starring Esther Williams, the 1940s water-ballet beauty (see p24).

2 CocoWalk
MAP G3 ■ 3015 Grand Ave
■ www.cocowalk.net

This compact, two-story center is the heart of Coconut Grove Village, and features some good shopping, dining, and entertainment (see p110). The atmosphere is, in fact, that of a village. People hang out, zipping by on in-line skates and bikes, and checking each other out, and there's often live music happening right in the middle of it all. The main attraction in the evening is probably the large multiplex cinema.

3 Vizcaya Museum and Gardens

A historic and beautiful place; this icon of the city's cultural life is not to be missed (see pp20–21).

4 Biltmore Hotel
MAP F3

George Merrick was one of the visionaries who made Florida into what it is; this lavish hotel stands as a monument to his taste and grand ideas. Herculean pillars line the grand lobby, and from the terrace you can survey the largest hotel swimming pool in the country. Johnny Weismuller, the first movie Tarzan, used to teach swimming here, and the likes of Al Capone, Judy Garland, and the Duke and Duchess of Windsor came here in its heyday. Weekly tours of the hotel and grounds depart from the front desk (see p24).

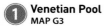

Biltmore Hotel, a Coral Gables hallmark

5 Miracle Mile

MAP F3–G3 ▪ Coral Way between Douglas and Le Jeune

In 1940, a developer hyped the town's main shopping street by naming it Miracle Mile. Colorful canopies adorn shops as prim and proper as their clientele. Note Merrick's Colonnade Building, at No. 169, with its splendid rotunda, fountain, and Corinthian columns; and, on nearby Salzedo Street, the Old Police and Fire Station (c.1939), with its square-jawed sculpted firemen.

COCONUT GROVE VILLAGE WEST

The West Grove neighborhood was established in the 1880s by Afro-Bahamian settlers. One settler, E.W.F. Stirrup, became one of Miami's first black millionaires and built over 100 "shotgun houses" for rent or sale to Bahamian families. From 1925, this thriving community was deprived of resources because of racial segregation policies, and gradually broke down. Since 2000, much has been done to revitalize this culturally rich area – local people have been working with (and sometimes against) developers to build affordable homes and celebrate Bahamian culture.

6 International Villages

MAP G4

Merrick's architectural flights of fancy still add a special grace note to beautiful, upscale Coral Gables. All are private homes, but you can drive by and take in their unique charms (see also pp24–5).

The house at Barnacle Historic State Park

Asian collection, Lowe Art Museum

7 Lowe Art Museum

With more than 17,500 pieces, Greater Miami's finest art museum boasts solid collections of ancient and modern world art (see pp26–7).

8 Barnacle Historic State Park

MAP G3 ▪ 3485 Main Highway, Coconut Grove ▪ 305-442-6866 ▪ Open 9am–5pm daily; closed Tue and national holidays ▪ 1-hour tours at 10 & 11:30am, 1 & 2:30pm ▪ Adm ▪ www.floridastateparks.org

Hidden away from the highway by a tropical hardwood hammock (mound) in Barnacle Historic State Park, this is Dade County's oldest home. It was designed and built in 1891 by Commodore Ralph Munroe, who made his living as a boat builder and a wrecker (salvager). In fact, wood from shipwrecks was used to build the house, and it was inventively laid out to allow the circulation of air, all-important in the days before air-conditioning. Rooms are packed with old family heirlooms, old tools, and wonderful early appliances.

9 The Kampong
MAP G4 ▪ 4013 Douglas Rd
▪ 305-442-7169 ▪ Open 9am–
4pm Wed–Fri, 10am–3pm Sat
▪ www.ntbg.org

Just southwest of Downtown, Coconut Grove is one of Miami's lesser-visited attractions, a vast botanical garden created by explorer and horticulturist David Fairchild. He bought the estate in 1916, spending the next 40 years developing a collection of more than 5,000 tropical flowers, fruit trees, and plants, with an emphasis on Asia. The site includes the Fairchild-Sweeney House, built in 1928 in a combination of Spanish and Southeast Asian styles.

Arched entrance into the Kampong

10 Dinner Key
MAP G3 ▪ 5 Bayshore Dr

The name derives from the early days when settlers had picnics here. In the 1930s, Pan American Airways transformed Dinner Key into the busiest seaplane base in the US. It was also the departure point for Amelia Earhart's doomed round-the-world flight in 1937. You can still see the airline's sleek Streamline Moderne terminal, housing the Miami City Hall; the hangars where seaplanes were harbored are now mostly boatyards. The marina here is the most prestigious in Miami, and berths many luxurious yachts.

A TOUR OF COCONUT GROVE VILLAGE

MORNING

This walk is designed for Wednesday to Monday, because it begins with a tour of the **Barnacle Historic State Park**. Try to get there for the 10am tour, and take note of the distinctive roof, which gives the house its name.
As you exit, turn left and go down to the corner of Devon Road to enjoy the beautiful Mission-style Plymouth Congregational Church, built in 1916. If they're open, pop into the back gardens. Walk back along Main Highway several blocks to No. 3500, the Coconut Grove Playhouse, which although not used, is a handsome Mediterranean Revival building that dominates the corner at Charles Avenue. Continue along Main Highway to the next street, then stop for lunch and top-notch people-watching at the ever-busy **Green Street Café** *(see p110)*.

AFTERNOON

After lunch, walk up Commodore Plaza to visit the **Midori Gallery** *(see p112)*. Afterwards, continue on to Grand Avenue and turn right; go down a few blocks to the major intersection and cross the street into the shopping mecca **CocoWalk** *(see p107)*. On the next block, Rice Street, look up to admire the fanciful facade of The Streets of Mayfair mall *(2911 Grand Avenue)*. To finish off your tour, visit nearby **Bombay Darbar** *(see p113)* for dinner. This Indian restaurant serves some of the best curries and kebabs in Miami.

See map on pp106–7

Special Places and Events

Stacked shelves at Books and Books

① Books and Books
One of Greater Miami's best bookstores, this is set amid graceful arcades *(see p112)*.

② Johnny Rockets
MAP F3 ▪ 5701 Sunset Dr, Coral Gables

This 1950s-style diner near Coral Gables is always jumping. Order a burger and fries and watch the young local crowds go by.

③ Green Street Café
MAP G3 ▪ 3110 Commodore Plaza, Coconut Grove ▪ 305-444-0244

Almost always crowded, this corner venue is another prime people-watching spot in the Grove.

④ CocoWalk
A compact shopping and entertainment center in the heart of Coconut Grove – always something or someone to catch the eye *(see p107)*.

⑤ Watsco Center
MAP G3 ▪ 1245 Dauer Dr, Coral Gables ▪ 305-284-8686

This modern arena on the University of Miami campus seats 8,000 for a variety of events, from college basketball to rock concerts.

⑥ Coconut Grove Arts Festival
MAP G3 ▪ Third weekend in Feb ▪ Throughout the Grove, especially Bayshore and Peacock Parks ▪ www.coconutgroveartsfest.com

Perhaps Greater Miami's best such festival, attracting throngs of visitors who come to eat, drink, listen to concerts in Peacock Park, and browse among 300 arts and crafts booths.

⑦ Miami International Orchid Show
Late Feb/early Mar ▪ www.sforchid.com

Florida has become one of the world centers for the orchid industry. More than half a million blooms are displayed at this show, which has a different theme every year.

⑧ Miami-Bahamas Goombay Festival
MAP G3 ▪ First weekend in Jun ▪ Throughout the Grove

A Bahamian party that includes a parade, Island food, Caribbean music, and *junkanoo* dancers parading through the streets. It claims to be the biggest African-American heritage festival in the US.

⑨ Columbus Day Regatta
MAP G3 ▪ Mid-Oct ▪ Coral Reef Yacht Club to Elliot Key ▪ www.columbusdayregatta.net

Some 600 boats take part in this celebration of the explorer.

⑩ King Mango Strut
MAP G3 ▪ Last week of Dec ▪ Starts at Main Hwy & Commodore Plaza, Coconut Grove ▪ www.kingmangostrut.com

Outrageous tradition that sends up the year's events and celebrities, harking back to the days when the Grove was a haven for intellectuals and eccentrics. The party climaxes with a concert and dance in Peacock Park.

See map on pp106–7

Walks, Drives, and Historic Sites

1 Miracle Mile
Though not really quite a mile, nor particularly miraculous, this street and the parallel ones are mostly about nice shops and elegant eateries, with some architectural interest (see p108).

2 Coconut Grove Village
MAP G3
This is a lovely place to walk (see p109), with its vibrant community centered around CocoWalk.

3 Merrick Villages
Driving around Coral Gables to take in these charming residences, done up in the styles of various national and regional cultures, will take perhaps a couple of hours to fully appreciate (see pp24–5).

4 Barnacle Historic State Park
This unusual house is the area's oldest, built in 1891 (see p108).

5 Biltmore Hotel
Inimitably beautiful and grand, this is one of the world's most gorgeous hotels, another Merrick gem opened in 1926 (see p107).

6 Vizcaya Museum and Gardens
A recreation of a 16th-century Italian villa complemented by beautiful, formal gardens (see pp20–21).

7 Congregational Church
Merrick's deliciously Baroque paean to his father, a Congregational minister, was Coral Gables' first church and remains the city's most beautiful to this day (see p25).

8 Venetian Pool
Considered the world's most beautiful public swimming pool. You could spend half a day enjoying its charms. Note that children under the age of three are not allowed (see p24).

9 Coral Gables Merrick House
MAP G3 ■ 907 Coral Way ■ 305-460-5361 ■ House open 1–4pm most Sun; grounds 8am–sunset daily ■ Adm
The restored boyhood home of George Merrick (see p25) is remarkably modest compared to the grandeur of the dreams he realized. The city of Coral Gables took its name from this house. The stone to build it was quarried from what is now the Venetian Pool. Currently under renovation, the house can still be admired from outside.

10 Lowe Art Museum
Originally founded in 1950, the Lowe Art Museum continues to grow. It showcases ancient Egyptian, Greco-Roman, Asian, and American art through the 17th century to contemporary European and American art (see pp26–7).

Looking back across the water to the east facade of Villa Vizcaya

Boutiques

1 Modernism Gallery
MAP G3 ■ 770 Ponce de Leon Blvd, Coral Gables

One of the country's top dealers in ultracool furniture, lighting fixtures, and accessories, including Art Deco.

2 Palm Produce Resortwear
MAP G3 ■ 3015 Grand Ave, #220, Coconut Grove

Loose and colorful lifestyle clothing in natural fabrics, and frivolous designs for both men and women.

3 L Boutique
MAP G3 ■ 133 Giralda Ave ■ 305-441-2772

A hidden gem in Coral Gables. Great selection of stylish women's clothing, with a fabulous line in patterned dresses and jumpsuits.

4 Books and Books
MAP G3 ■ 265 Aragon Ave, Coral Gables

One of a chain of stores across the state, this bookshop specializes in arts and literature, and books on Florida. Here there's a great café, frequent poetry readings, and book signings.

5 Midori Gallery
MAP G3 ■ 3168 Commodore Plaza, Coconut Grove

Exquisite, museum-quality Chinese and Japanese ceramics, lacquers and ivories, some as old as the Eastern Han Dynasty, 25–220 AD.

6 White House Black Market
MAP G3 ■ 350 San Lorenzo Ave, Suite 2130

A rarified range of women's fashion. Elegant, sequined evening gowns, smart tailored suits, peignoirs, and underthings.

7 Golden Triangle
MAP G3 ■ 2308 Galiano St, Coral Gables

Funky boutique stocking imported Asian items: incense, jewelry, Tibetan bowls, Buddha statues, beautiful clothing, crystals, and more.

8 Fashionista
MAP G3 ■ 3135 Commodore Plaza, Coconut Grove

This is the place to pick up designer merchandise, albeit slightly worn, for a fraction of the price.

9 Azul Coconut Grove
MAP G3 ■ 3015 Grand Ave, Coconut Grove

Offering a range of unique brands, this fashion boutique perfectly balances classic styles with latest trends.

10 Essence Boutique
MAP G3 ■ 78 Miracle Mile, Coral Gables ■ 305-448-0689

Upscale women's attire, with trendy purses, shoes, and swimwear, and quirky jewelry too.

Ceramic and ivory, Midori Gallery

Trendy Restaurants

PRICE CATEGORIES

For a three-course meal for one with half a bottle of wine (or equivalent meal), taxes, and extra charges.

$ under $35 $$ $35–$70 $$$ over $70

1 Pascal's on Ponce
MAP G3 ■ 2611 Ponce de Leon Blvd, Coral Gables ■ 305-444-2024 ■ $$

A perfect place for a romantic meal, with exquisite French cuisine by chef Pascal Oudin, fine linens, beautiful table settings, and attentive staff.

2 Palme d'Or
MAP F3 ■ 1200 Anastasia Ave, Coral Gables ■ 305-913-3201 ■ $$$

This restaurant offers an authentic fine dining experience. Enjoy the exquisite French cuisine prepared by the Michelin-starred chef Gregory Pugin.

3 Christy's
MAP G3 ■ 3101 Ponce de Leon Blvd, Coral Gables ■ 305-446-1400 ■ $$

A local favorite since its opening in 1978, this restaurant has been made a landmark by politicians, CEOs, and celebrities. Aged steak, fresh seafood, and award-winning caesar salad.

4 Berries in the Grove
MAP G3 ■ 2884 SW 27th Ave ■ 305-448-2111 ■ $

Locals have embraced this eatery, which captures the best of Florida's sunshine and healthy cuisine – from a pizza to a tropical fruit smoothie.

5 Bombay Darbar
MAP G3 ■ 2901 Florida Ave, Coconut Grove ■ 786-444-7272 ■ $$

Regarded as Miami's best Indian restaurant. Kebabs and curries are what elevate this establishment.

6 Titanic Brewing Company
MAP G3 ■ 5813 Ponce de Leon Blvd, Coral Gables ■ 305-667-2537 ■ $

Lift a pint of homemade brew and sample crawfish or calamari snacks.

7 Ortanique on the Mile
MAP G3 ■ 278 Miracle Mile, Coral Gables (next to Actor's Playhouse) ■ 305-446-7710 ■ $$

Dine on Caribbean cuisine in this cozy restaurant. Try the Bahamian grouper or the jerked pork chop with guava for a taste of the islands.

8 Caffe Abbracci
MAP G3 ■ 318 Aragon Ave, Coral Gables ■ 305-441-0700 ■ $$

Owned by Nino Pernetti, this restaurant offers a Mediterranean ambience that complements its Italian comfort food. The menu has a variety of desserts as well as an extensive wine list.

Sophisticated setting, Bizcaya

9 Bizcaya
MAP G3 ■ 3300 SW 27th Ave, Coconut Grove ■ 305-644-4675 ■ $$

Housed in the Ritz Carlton, this gourmet restaurant serves grilled steaks and seafood with flair. Dishes on the menu include lamb *osso bucco* with imported mini ravioli.

10 Le Bouchon du Grove
MAP G3 ■ 3430 Main Highway, Coconut Grove ■ 305-448-6060 ■ $$

Transporting diners to Paris for twenty years, this cozy bistrot is renowned for its traditional French cuisine. It serves breakfast, lunch, and dinner.

See map on pp106–7

🔟 South of Coconut Grove

Heading south from Miami's main events, once you get past the nondescript suburbs, you enter tracts of citrus groves and tropical nurseries. The general atmosphere changes too – a bit more traditional and Old South. There is a great range of shopping opportunities, museums, parks, gardens, and zoos. And you'll discover educational attractions for kids and adults alike, including Biscayne National Underwater Park.

Fairchild Tropical Botanic Garden

SOUTH OF COCONUT GROVE

1 **Top 10 Sights**
see pp115–17

1 **Places to Eat**
see p119

1 **Regional Souvenir Shops**
see p118

Patricia & Phillip Frost Art Museum

WESTCHESTER

CORAL WAY

Fairchild Tropical Botanic Garden

Montgomery Botanical Center

KENDALL

PALMETTO BAY

Gold Coast Railroad Museum

CORAL REEF DR

Charles Deering Estate

Zoo Miami

CUTLER BAY

Fruit & Spice Park

Safari Edventure

PRINCETON

Coral Castle

Mangrove Preserve

Biscayne National Underwater Park

Biscayne Bay

HOMESTEAD

0 km   5
0 miles   5

1 Fairchild Tropical Botanic Garden

MAP G4 ▪ 10901 Old Cutler Rd ▪ 305-667-1651 ▪ Open 9:30am–4:30pm daily ▪ Adm ▪ www.fairchildgarden.org

This dizzyingly beautiful tropical paradise was established in 1938 and also serves as a botanical research institute. Around a series of man-made lakes stands one of the world's largest collections of palm trees, as well as countless other wonderful trees and plants. During a tram tour, guides describe how plants are used in the manufacture of everything from Chanel No. 5 to golf balls.

2 Fruit & Spice Park

MAP E5 ▪ 24801 Redland Rd (SW 187th Ave), Homestead ▪ 305-247-5727 ▪ Open 9am–5pm daily ▪ Adm ▪ Guided tours ▪ redlandfruit andspice.com

This 30-acre (12-ha) botanical park is devoted to tropical plants, such as citrus fruits, grapes, bananas, herbs, spices, nuts, and bamboo. The astonishing number of varieties on display include a selection of poisonous species and hundreds of bamboo and banana varieties. A wonderful store enables you to stock up your cupboards with many unusual fruit products.

3 Montgomery Botanical Center

MAP G4 ▪ 11901 Old Cutler Road, Coral Gables ▪ 305-667-3800, call ahead to book a visit ▪ www.montgomerybotanical.org

Formerly a private estate, this 120-acre park was created by Robert and Nell Montgomery, founders of the Fairchild Botanic Garden. Its aim is to advance science, education, conservation and knowledge of tropical plants for garden design. The vast collection of tropical plants focuses on palms and cycads from around the world.

Bananas, Fruit & Spice Park

Coral Castle, carved from coral rock

4 Coral Castle

MAP E6 ▪ 28655 South Dixie Hwy ▪ 305-248-6345 ▪ Open 8am–6pm Sun–Thu, 8am–8pm Fri–Sat ▪ Adm ▪ www.coralcastle.com

A castle it isn't, but a conundrum it is. From 1920 to 1940, Latvian immigrant Edward Leedskalnin built this mysterious pile as a Valentine to a girl who had jilted him in 1913. No one knows how he single-handedly quarried and transported the 1,100 tons of tough coral rock, carved all the enormous chunks into monumental shapes, and set them all into place so flawlessly. One 9-ton gate is so exquisitely balanced that it opens with the pressure of your little finger.

5 Safari Edventure

MAP E5 ▪ 23700 SW 142nd Ave, Miami ▪ Open 10am–5pm Wed–Sun ▪ www.safariedventure.com

This family-friendly non-profit animal sanctuary specializes in hands-on experiences. Get up-close to around 120 species, including sloths, kangaroos, monkeys lemurs, and alligators. The site has a sunken rainforest plus butterfly and hummingbird gardens.

Stone House, Charles Deering Estate

6 Charles Deering Estate
MAP F4 ▪ 16701 SW 72nd Ave, at SW 167th St & Old Cutler Rd ▪ 305-235-1668 ▪ Open 10am–4pm daily ▪ Adm ▪ www.deeringestate.org

Right on Biscayne Bay, the estate contains two significant architectural works: Richmond Cottage, built in 1896 as the area's first inn, and a large Mediterranean Revival "Stone House," which was built in 1922.

7 Zoo Miami
MAP E5 ▪ 12400 SW 152nd St ▪ 305-251-0400 ▪ Open 9:30am–5:30pm daily ▪ Adm ▪ www.zoomiami.org

The zoo works a great deal with endangered species. Zookeepers give talks at feeding times (see p45).

8 Biscayne National Underwater Park
MAP G5 ▪ SW 328th St Homestead ▪ 305-230-7275 ▪ Open 9am–5pm daily ▪ www.nps.gov/bisc

Biscayne National Underwater Park is 95 percent water, therefore most visitors enter it by private boat. Otherwise, the Dante Fascell Visitor Center at Convoy Point is the only place in the national park you can drive to and, from there, you have several boating options. The concession offers canoe rentals, glass-bottom boat tours, snorkel trips, scuba trips, and transportation to the island for campers. There's also a picturesque boardwalk that takes you along the shoreline out to the rock jetty beside the boat channel heading to the bay.

9 Patricia & Phillip Frost Art Museum
MAP F3 ▪ 10975 SW 17th St ▪ 305-348-2890 ▪ Open 10am–5pm Tue–Sat, noon–5pm Sun ▪ 1-hour tours by reservation ▪ www.thefrost.fiu.edu

The museum specializes in Latin American and 20th-century American art and presents six to eight major exhibitions each year. The Martin Z. Margulies Sculpture Park displays 69 works in a variety of media that are distributed

A tiger at Zoo Miami

throughout the 26.5 acres (8 ha) of the FIU (Florida International University) campus – a wonderfully rich and important representation of modern work. It is recognized nationally as one of the world's great collections of sculpture and the largest on a university campus. It includes major pieces by Dubuffet, Miro, Nevelson, Calder, Noguchi, and Serra.

Engine, Gold Coast Railroad Museum

⑩ Gold Coast Railroad Museum
MAP E4 ■ 12450 SW 152nd St ■ 305-253-0063 ■ Open 10am–4pm Mon–Fri, 11am–4pm Sat–Sun ■ Adm ■ www.gcrm.org

The museum was started in 1957 by a group of Miamians who were trying to save threatened pieces of Florida history. Some of the oldest items in the collection are the "Ferdinand Magellan," a private railroad car built for President Franklin Roosevelt; the FEC engine that pulled a rescue train out from Marathon after the 1935 hurricane; and the 113 locomotive built in 1913. The Edwin Link is a small-gauge children's railroad.

HURRICANE COUNTRY
One in ten of the hurricanes that form in the North Atlantic hits Florida, which means an average of one big storm every two years. On September 10, 2017, Hurricane Irma was one such storm, measuring 4 on the Saffir-Simpson Scale by the time it made landfall in Florida. The worst is a 5, like the one that hit the Keys on Labor Day in 1935, destroying the Flagler bridge.

DEERING ESTATE WALK

▶ MORNING

To get to the **Charles Deering Estate**, drive south from Miami on Highway 1 (Dixie Highway) and turn left on SW 168th Street. Follow it until it dead-ends at the estate on SW 72nd Avenue. A full tour of the grounds will take three to four hours. Follow the Entrance Trail to begin, and as you emerge from the mangroves you will encounter a splendid vista of Biscayne Bay. Note the water level marker showing the inundation caused by Hurricane Andrew in 1992. Richmond Cottage, the original structure here, was built as an inn in 1896. It was destroyed by Andrew, but has since been replicated. The elegant Stone House next door contains bronze and copper doors, portraits of the Deering family, a celebrated wine cellar, and more besides. Head over to the Carriage House, where you can see a vintage gas pump. If you have time, take the Main Nature Trail, which crosses a handsome coral rock bridge, built in 1918. Finally, walk out through the estate's historic Main Entrance, with its coral rock pillars, and wood and iron gates.

AFTERNOON

Picnicking on the grounds is a possibility, and some facilities are provided. Or, for a hearty lunch, take a short drive north to **Guadalajara** *(see p119)*. To make a full day's outing, head south along Highway 1 to the eccentric **Coral Castle** *(see p115)*.

See map on p114

Regional Souvenir Shops

1 Brighton Collectibles
MAP F4 ▪ The Falls Shopping Center, US Highway 1, 8888 SW 136th St ▪ 305-254-0044

Shop here for a fine collection of home gifts, leather handbags, picture frames, watches, and jewelry.

Bloomingdales store, The Falls

2 The Falls Shopping Center
MAP F4 ▪ US Highway 1, SW 136th St ▪ 305-255-4570 ▪ www.simon.com/mall/the-falls

This is one of the largest open-air shopping, dining, and entertainment complexes in the country. There are over 100 stores set in a picturesque waterscape with tropical foliage.

3 Papyrus
MAP F4 ▪ The Falls Shopping Center, US Highway 1, SW 136th St ▪ 305-252-3888

On offer are a large assortment of stationery, key chains, rings, pen and pencil gift sets, and letter openers.

4 Little Havana Gift Shop
MAP J3 ▪ 1522 SW 8th St ▪ 786-768-1170

Stocked with Cuban items, this shop also has objects such as magnets, bags, pens, and other souvenirs. Most items are locally made.

5 Guayaberas Etc.
MAP F3 ▪ 8870 SW 40th St ▪ 305-485-1114

This store stocks classic shirts in stylish linen and comfortable cotton for men, women, and children.

6 Miami Twice
MAP F3 ▪ 6562 SW 40th St ▪ 305-666-0127

Along with vintage clothing and jewelry, antique-hunters should visit Miami Twice to discover Art Deco items and other treasure.

7 O'Sew Crafty
MAP F5 ▪ 12315 SW 224th St ▪ 305-258-2949

This adorable gift shop sells craft items handmade by local artisans, including toys, embroidery, and crochet. You can even pick up some tips on how to make some simple inexpensive presents to take home.

8 Claire's Boutique
MAP F5 ▪ 20505 South Dixie Hwy, Southland Mall ▪ 305-251-2307

Great gift items from earrings and bracelets to hair accessories and purses are sold at this great boutique.

9 Island Colors
MAP F5 ▪ Cauley Square, 12309 SW 224th St ▪ 305-258-2565

This cultural cottage experience produces authentic paintings, sculptures, iron works, and souvenirs from Haiti and Africa.

10 The Aviary
MAP E5 ▪ 22400 Old Dixie Hwy ▪ www.aviarybirdshop.com

Here's the place for you if you've finally decided you must sport a macaw or cockatoo on your shoulder. Plus, you can buy your new pet a Tiki Hut cage and all the seed and accoutrements it will need. A wonderful place to visit, laid out like a tropical garden.

Canary, The Aviary

Places to Eat

PRICE CATEGORIES

For a three-course meal for one with half a bottle of wine (or equivalent meal), taxes, and extra charges.

$ under $35 $$ $35–$70 $$$ over $70

1 Shorty's BBQ
MAP F4 ▪ 9200 S Dixie Hwy ▪ 305-670-7732 ▪ $

This South Florida minichain, set up in 1951 by E. L. "Shorty" Allen, is known for its barbecue chicken, pulled pork, and sumptuous baby-back ribs.

2 Whip N Dip Ice Cream
MAP G4 ▪ 1407 Sunset Dr ▪ 305-665-2565 ▪ $

Hard-to-resist cakes and ice cream, made with locally sourced ingredients and created on site; think banana nut chip, pineapple sorbet, and chocolate cheesecake flavors.

3 Robert Is Here
MAP E6 ▪ 19200 SW 344th St, Homestead ▪ 305-246-1592 ▪ $

This legendary fruit stand (now a huge roadside store) has specialized in locally grown rare and exotic fruits since 1959. Also serves milkshakes and smoothies.

4 Black Point Ocean Grill
MAP F5 ▪ 24775 SW 87th Ave, Cutler Bay ▪ 305-258-3918 ▪ $

Lively restaurant overlooking Black Point Marina and Black Creek, with a menu of fresh seafood, hand-cut steaks, salads, and sandwiches. Alfresco seating available.

5 Guadalajara
MAP F4 ▪ 8461 SW 132nd St, Pinecrest ▪ 786-242-4444 ▪ $

Home-cooked Mexican fare in a characterful locale. Try dipping a tortilla in a *queso fundido* (cheese fondue). The portions are huge.

6 Two Chefs
MAP F4 ▪ 8287 South Dixie Hwy ▪ 305-663-2100 ▪ $$

American and contemporary cuisine with international influences are served in a bistro-style setting.

7 The Melting Pot
MAP F4 ▪ 11520 SW Sunset Dr ▪ 305-279-8816 ▪ $$

A relaxed atmosphere with private tables. The menu ranges from vegetarian dishes to filet mignon.

8 Sweet Delights
MAP F5 ▪ 12690 SW 280th St ▪ 305-204-2544 ▪ $

Best place in South Miami to buy Key lime pie, with at least 16 different varieties to try – customers are encouraged to taste samples first.

Lovely bay views at Red Fish Grill

9 Red Fish Grill
MAP G4 ▪ 9610 Old Cutler Rd ▪ 305-668-8788 ▪ $$

One of Miami's most romantic spots, nestled amid the tropical magic of Matheson Hammock Park. Freshly caught fish and other dishes are lovingly prepared with Caribbean flair.

10 Redland Ranch
MAP E5 ▪ 14655 SW 232nd St, South Miami ▪ 786-493-2805 ▪ Closed Mon & Tue ▪ $

Tropical produce store with a cult following, offering juices, shakes, smoothies, sandwiches, and fruits.

See map on p114

⭐10 The Keys

Helmet, Mel Fisher Maritime Museum

The Florida Keys are a string of wild, variegated gems hung in a necklace of liquid turquoise. These islands still have abundant wildlife, including unique flora and fauna, as evidenced by the many parks and family attractions focusing on encounters with nature. Even so, at least 20 different species of Keys plant and animal life are endangered or threatened. This is a place for outdoor activities: watersports of all kinds, sportfishing, and hiking through the nature preserves and virgin tropical forests.

Along the only route (US 1) that takes you from the mainland all the way out to Key West, you'll find everything from plush resorts to roadside stands selling wonderful home-grown produce.

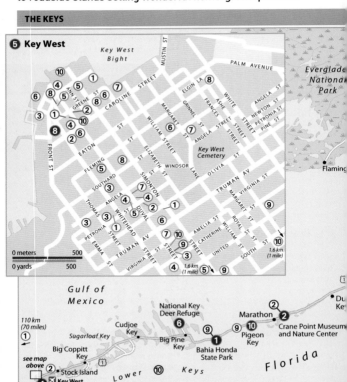

THE KEYS

5 Key West

1 Bahia Honda State Park

MAP B6 ▪ Bahia Honda Key, MM 37 oceanside ▪ 305-872-3210 ▪ Open 8am–sunset daily ▪ Adm ▪ www. floridastateparks.org/bahiahonda

This protected area boasts the finest beaches in the Keys – and is voted among the best in the US. Brilliantly white sand is backed by tropical forest crossed by nature trails.

2 Crane Point Museum and Nature Center

MAP C6 ▪ MM 50.5 bayside ▪ 305-743-9100 ▪ Open 9am–5pm Mon–Sat, noon–5pm Sun ▪ Adm ▪ www.crane point.net

You can see a 600-year-old dugout canoe, remnants of pirate ships, a simulated coral reef cave, and the Bellarmine jug (c.1580), a shipwreck artifact in almost perfect condition. There's also a gift shop and the colorful Marathon Wild Bird Center.

John Pennekamp Coral Reef State Park

3 John Pennekamp Coral Reef State Park

MAP D5 ▪ MM 102.5 oceanside ▪ 305-451-6300 ▪ Open 8am–5pm daily ▪ Adm ▪ www.pennekamppark.com

The park is known for its fabulous coral reef life. You can also rent canoes, dinghies, or motorboats, as well as snorkeling and scuba gear, or choose a glass-bottom boat ride. Most destinations are actually in the neighboring Florida Keys (Key Largo) National Marine Sanctuary. The shallow waters of Dry Rocks are especially good for snorkeling, as is the nearby Molasses Reef.

4 Key West Wildlife Center

MAP A6 ▪ 1801 White St, Key West ▪ Open 9am–5pm daily; closed Wed ▪ www.keywestwildlifecenter.org

This wildlife rehabilitation center and nature reserve, located in a 7-acre- (3-ha-) Indigenous Park in Key West, provides refuge for marine and land mammals, wild birds, sea turtles, and tortoises. Wander the pleasant, meandering nature trail.

Miami

Homestead

Key Largo

Key Largo   John Pennekamp Coral Reef State Park

Wild Bird Rehabilitation Center

Islamorada

Indian Key Historic State Park

Keys

Straits of Florida

0 km   12
0 miles   12

Key West Museum of Art and History

5 Key West

Rich in breathtaking beauty and in history, the self-styled Conch (pronounced "konk") Republic seems truly a world apart from the rest of the United States (see pp32–3).

6 National Key Deer Refuge

MAP B6 ■ MM 30.5 bayside ■ 305-872-0774 ■ Open 9am–4pm daily

Spanning a varied landscape of pine forest, mangroves, tropical hardwood hammocks, and fresh- and salt water wetlands, this refuge is home to 23 endangered and threatened species of flora and fauna, including the endangered Key deer. As a consequence of poaching and loss of habitats, fewer than 50 of these diminutive creatures were left until this refuge was established in 1957. Now there are estimated to be about 600. Drive very slowly and don't feed them.

7 Indian Key Historic State Park

MAP C5 ■ MM 78.5 oceanside ■ 305-664-2540 for ferry service ■ Open 8am–sunset daily ■ www.florida stateparks.org/indiankey

Tiny Indian Key has a surprisingly large amount of history for its size (10.5 acres/4.25 ha). An ancient Native American site, it was settled in 1831 by Captain J. Houseman, an opportunistic wrecker. In 1840 Seminoles attacked, killing the settlers. The Key was abandoned, and today only the outlines of the village remain, overgrown by vegetation. These are the descendants of plants belonging to Dr. Henry Perrine, a botanist who was killed in the raid.

8 Mel Fisher Maritime Museum

MAP A6 ■ 200 Greene St, Key West ■ 305-294-2633 ■ Open 8:30am–5pm Mon–Fri, 9:30am–5pm Sat–Sun ■ Adm ■ www.melfisher.org

The maritime museum brings you the Age of Discovery, from the late 15th to the mid-18th centuries, when Europeans explored what was to them the "New World." Their exploits, their commerce, and their impact on the native inhabitants of the Americas can be understood in the artifacts in this museum's collection. Its four ships include the *St. John's Wreck*, constructed in 1560, and the *Henrietta Marie*, an English galleon that sank off the Florida Keys in 1700.

THE KEYS: MYTH AND MAGIC

The very name conjures up visions of windswept seascapes and wild goings-on: Humphrey Bogart and Lauren Bacall in the classic melodrama, *Key Largo*; some of the greatest US writers (Ernest Hemingway, Tennessee Williams, et al.) finding their muses where the US meets the Caribbean; and a free, unfettered lifestyle too good to be true.

⑨ Florida Keys Wild Bird Rehabilitation Center

MAP C5 ▪ MM 93.6, bayside ▪ Open sunrise–sunset daily ▪ Donation ▪ www.keepthemflying.org

This refuge for native and migratory birds comprises a bird hospital and education center, and a bird sanctuary – 12 acres (5 ha) of wetlands providing a natural habitat for over 120 resident rescued birds, and other flourishing native flora and fauna.

Egret, Florida Keys Wild Bird Rehabilitation Center

⑩ Pigeon Key

MAP B6 ▪ Ferry depot at MM 47 oceanside ▪ 305-743-5999 ▪ Open 9:30am–4pm daily ▪ Adm ▪ www.pigeonkey.net

This was the site of the work camp for those who built Henry M. Flagler's Overseas Railroad Bridge, described as the eighth wonder of the world when completed in 1912. A marine research foundation has been established in the old buildings. To get to the island, walk or take the ferry.

Bird's-eye view of Pigeon Key

A DAY'S WALK ON KEY WEST

▶ **MORNING**

Begin at about 10am. Start at the Southernmost Point in continental US, overlooking the Atlantic at the intersection of Whitehead and South streets, where the marker informs you that Cuba is only 90 miles (144 km) away. Then head up Whitehead to the **Lighthouse Museum** *(see p33)* and climb its 88 steps for a great overview of the island and beyond. Next stop is the **Hemingway Home** *(see p32)*, at No. 907; here you can take in a nostalgic trip through the writer's life as a Conch. Then move on to the **Green Parrot Bar** *(see p130)*, at No. 601 Whitehead, to admire its age-old funkiness and have a drink before lunch. From here, head over to Duval Street, to **Mangoes** restaurant *(see p131)*, at No. 700, for a great lunch and stellar people-watching.

AFTERNOON

Admire the Spanish Colonial facade of the San Carlos Institute, and, on the next block up, the lovely stained-glass windows of St. Paul's Episcopal Church. At No. 322, visit the Oldest House Museum and Garden. Now things might get very "Key West," as you climb to the third floor of the **Bull and Whistle Bar** *(see p130)* to find the **Garden of Eden** *(see p57)* and see who's sunning themselves in this clothing-optional bar. Farther along stop at historic **Sloppy Joe's** *(see p130)*. By now, it should be time for the famous sunset celebration, so head down to Mallory Square *(see p32)*.

See map on pp120–21 ←

Nature Preserves

1 Key Largo Hammock Botanical State Park

MAP D5 ▪ 1 mile N of US 1, on Route 905, oceanside ▪ 305-451-1202 ▪ Open sunrise–sunset daily ▪ Adm

The largest remaining tropical West Indian hardwood and mangrove hammock is a refuge for protected indigenous flora and fauna.

2 Crane Point Museum and Nature Center

Walk the nature trails to Florida Bay and check out the Crane Point Museum and Nature Center and the Adderly Town Historic Site *(see p121)*.

3 Crocodile Lake Wildlife Refuge

MAP D5 ▪ 10750 County Road 905, Key Largo ▪ 305-451-4223 ▪ Open 9am–4pm

Part of the United States National Wildlife Refuge System, this crocodile refuge is itself closed to the public, but on site there is an information kiosk and a pleasant native pollinator garden for visitors to enjoy.

4 Florida Keys Wild Bird Rehabilitation Center

A safe haven for recovering Keys sea birds, including hawks, pelicans, herons, owls *(see p123)*.

5 John Pennekamp Coral Reef State Park

Most famous for its stunning offshore coral reef, where snorkeling, scuba diving, and glass-bottom boat rides are great favorites *(see p121)*.

6 Windley Key Fossil Reef State Geological Park

MAP C5 ▪ MM 84.9 bayside ▪ 305-664-2540 ▪ Open 8am–5pm Thu–Mon ▪ Adm

There are nature displays in the center of the park and trails lead into the railroad's old quarries, where you can discover exquisite pieces of fossilized brain coral and sea ferns.

7 Lignumvitae Key Botanical State Park

MAP C5 ▪ MM 78.5 bayside ▪ 305-664-9814 for ferry ▪ Open 9am–5pm Thu–Mon

Access is only by boat to this beautiful virgin hardwood forest home and gardens built by William Matheson.

8 Long Key State Park

MAP C6 ▪ MM 67.5 oceanside ▪ 305-664-2540 ▪ Open 8am–sunset daily ▪ Adm

Features include a boardwalk through a mangrove swamp where you can see waterbirds. Snorkeling is good in the shallow waters off the beach.

9 Bahia Honda State Park

Very heavily forested, with great nature trails. Fascinating snorkeling, too *(see p121)*.

10 Looe Key National Marine Sanctuary

MAP B6 ▪ MM 27.5 oceanside ▪ 305-872-3210

Looe Key Reef is one of the Keys' most spectacular coral reefs and is great for snorkeling and diving. Call about boat trips to the best spots.

Kids playing, John Pennekamp Park

Plants and Animals in the Keys

1 Coral
Although it appears to be insensate rock, coral is actually a living organism of various species, and a very fragile one at that, easily damaged by the slightest touch.

2 Palms
Although only a few species of palms are natives in the Keys – the royal palm, the sabal palm, the saw palmetto, and the thatch palm – a huge range of imported palms now adorn the islands.

3 Egrets
Often visible on the islands, and similar to herons, are the great egret, the snowy egret (distinguish-able by its black legs and yellow feet), and the reddish egret.

4 Double-Crested Cormorant
Notable for its S-curved neck, distinctive beak, and spectacular diving skills, this is one of the most fascinating of Keys birds.

5 White Ibis
Recognizable for its long, down-curving beak, this medium-sized white wading bird, numerous in Florida, was sacred to the Egyptians.

6 Key Deer
The diminutive Key deer are found primarily on Big Pine and No Name keys. Docile and endearing, these tiny animals have returned from the brink of extinction in the last 40 years.

7 Herons
These elegant long-legged birds include the great blue heron, the white phase heron, the little blue heron, the tricolored heron, the green-backed heron, and the black-crowned night heron.

Gumbo limbo, noted for its red bark

8 Gumbo Limbo Tree
Called the "tourist tree" due to its red and peeling bark, this unmis-takable species – a Florida native – is found all over the Keys.

9 Other Endangered Species
The Florida Keys conceal many endangered species. These include the American crocodile, the Key Largo wood rat and cotton mouse, Schaus swallowtail butterfly, and roseate spoonbill, all of which have either been hunted near to the point of extinction or lost their habitats due to human encroachment.

Roseate spoonbill in flight

10 Sea Turtles
These good-natured, long-lived creatures come in a wide variety of shapes and sizes. From the largest to the smallest they are the leather-back, the loggerhead, the green, the hawksbill, and the Ridley turtles.

See map on pp120–21

Sports Activities in the Keys

1 Swimming
Some of the best beaches in the world are in the Keys. Don't worry if the ocean temperature falls below the usual 79° F (26° C) – most hotels have heated swimming pools.

2 Fishing
Key West Fishing Club: www.keywestfishingclub.com
The Keys are a paradise for deep-sea fishing. With the Gulf Stream nearby, these waters offer the most varied fishing imaginable. Boat trips are easy to come by; try Key West Fishing Club.

3 Water-Skiing and Jet-Skiing
Island Water Sport: 305-296-1754
These more intense ways of enjoying the Keys' waters are available wherever there's a marina, especially in Key West and other developed tourist areas. Island Water Sport is one of the companies offering jet skis.

4 Boating and Sailing
The many dozens of marinas in the Keys are full of companies that are ready to rent you whatever kind of boat you would like – or to take you out, if that's what you prefer.

5 Cycling
There is no doubt that cycling is one of the best ways to see the Keys. The roads are fairly bike-friendly, especially in Key West, and bicycle rentals are readily available.

6 Tennis
Good tennis clubs can be found on just about every developed Key – on Islamorada at MM 76.8 bayside, Marathon at MM 53.5 oceanside, on Key West, of course, and elsewhere.

7 Golf
The Keys don't have as many courses as the rest of Florida, but there are several good ones, for example, Key Colony on Marathon Key at MM 53.5 oceanside, or a more expensive course on Key West.

8 Parasailing
Sebago Watersports: www.keywestsebago.com
As close to growing wings as you can get, parasailing is easy, safe, and unforgettable. Many companies, such as Sebago, offer the experience.

9 Windsurfing
With prevailing winds and calm, shallow waters that remain so for miles out to sea, the Keys are ideal for windsurfing. Most busy beaches up and down the islands have shops that rent the necessary equipment.

10 Snorkeling and Scuba Diving
Since the Keys are almost entirely surrounded by America's largest living coral reef, the underwater world is one of the areas main treats.

Scuba diving on the reef, Key Largo

Special Tours and Events

1 Dry Tortugas
**Key West Seaplane Adventures;
www.keywestseaplanecharters.com**
Take a plane or ferry to this undeveloped collection of islands, where the snorkeling is unbeatable *(see p133)*.

2 Sloan's Ghost Hunt
**MAP A6 ■ Tours depart each evening outside First Flight Restaurant and Bar, 301 Whitehead St, Key West
■ www.hauntedkeywest.com**
Discover the supernatural with a 90-minute stroll through the mysterious streets of Key West's Old Town.

3 Goombay Celebration
MAP A6 ■ Bahama Village, Key West
A celebration of Island culture and life. Held in mid-October, it usually merges with the Fantasy Fest.

Conch train outside Sloppy Joe's

4 Conch Tour Train
**MAP A6 ■ 303 Front St, Key West ■ 888-916-8687
■ www.conchtourtrain.com**
Key West's train tour is a must-do for first-time visitors. It gives an overview of the place and all sorts of insights into its history and culture.

5 Old Town Trolley Tour in Key West
**MAP A6 ■ 305-296-6688
■ www.trolleytours.com**
Jump aboard this orange and green trolley to see the sights of Key West. A ticket for the narrated tour allows you to hop on and off all day.

Fantasy Fest parade, Key West

6 Fantasy Fest
MAP A6 ■ Last 2 weeks in Oct
Held on Key West leading up to and including Halloween, this is a festival with a positive atmosphere *(see p75)*.

7 Annual Conch-Blowing Contest
Early March is when this traditional means of musical expression – or noise-making in less-skilled cases – fills the air over Key West.

8 New Year's Eve in Key West
In Key West, welcoming the New Year starts with the Last Sunset celebration at Mallory Square, followed by several local acts and fireworks on Blackwater Sound.

9 Seven-Mile Bridge Run
**MAP B6 ■ Marathon Key
■ 305-743-5417 ■ www.7mbrun.com**
In early- to mid-April, enthusiastic runners honor the bridge that joined all the Keys together by conquering it with their own two feet.

10 Hemingway Days
305-294-1136
Held in the middle of the low season, the third week of July (Hemingway's birthday was July 21st), this party is most loved by the locals, or "Conchs", who attend in great numbers . Hemingway look-alikes lead the celebrations and tributes to the island's most famous writer.

See map on pp120–21

Island Shopping

1 Besame Mucho
MAP A6 ▪ 315 Petronia St, Key West ▪ www.besame mucho.net
This boutique, in the Bahama Village neighborhood, sells lovely gifts such as candles, jewelry, and home decor.

2 The Gallery at Kona Kai Resort
MAP C5 ▪ MM 97.8 bayside, 97802 Overseas Highway (US 1) ▪ www. konakairesort.com
Impressive international artwork, including paintings by Sobran and Magni, powerful bronze sculptures, and fine Keys nature photography.

3 Sweets of Paradise
MAP A6 ▪ 291 Front St #5, Key West
Come here for heavenly, homemade sweets. The fudge is made with Belgian chocolate, and the Key lime pie on a stick is to die for.

African wood carvings, Archeo

4 Archeo
MAP A6 ▪ 1208 Duval St, Key West ▪ www.archeogallery.com
Rare African masks and wood carvings, plus stunning Persian rugs.

5 Kino Sandals
MAP A6 ▪ 107 Fitzpatrick St, Key West ▪ www.kinosandal factory.com
Sandal factory where every pair is an original design and handmade by artisans using natural leather uppers and natural rubber soles.

Kermit's Key West Key Lime Shoppe

6 Kermit's Key West Key Lime Shoppe
MAP A6 ▪ 200 Elizabeth St, Key West
This pretty little shop serves one of the tastiest Key lime pies in town, plus Key lime-flavor cookies, salsa, chutney, taffy, tea, and olive oil.

7 Key West Aloe
MAP A6 ▪ 419 Duval St, Key West ▪ www.keywestaloe.com
A company that has made their own all-natural products since 1971, without any animal testing.

8 Peppers of Key West
MAP A6 ▪ 602 Greene St, Key West ▪ www. peppersofkeywest.com
The shelves here are stacked with an astonishing array of spicy sauces to suit every palate; from fiery hot sauce and traditional Jerk season-ing, to peppery mustard and piquant salsa.

9 Old Road Gallery
MAP C5 ▪ 88888 Old Highway, Tavernier ▪ 305-852-8935
Peruse beach-oriented artworks crafted by local artists at this pleasant gallery, sculpture garden, and pottery studio.

10 Grand Vin
MAP A6 ▪ 1107 Duval St, Key West
If you are looking for great wines from around the world at good prices, and the chance to try many of them by the glass, this is the place. Sit out on the porch and enjoy.

→ *See map on pp120–21*

LGBT+ Venues

1 Bobby's Monkey Bar
MAP A6 ▪ 900 Simonton St, Key West ▪ 305-294-2655
Lively, colorful gay bar popular with both locals and visitors thanks to its friendly staff and offbeat events.

2 1 Saloon
MAP A6 ▪ 504 Petronia St, Key West
Raunchy gay leather bar, with a seedy but seductive atmosphere and friendly bartenders. Open 5pm–4am daily.

3 La-Te-Da
MAP A6 ▪ 1125 Duval St, Key West ▪ 305-296-6706
This upscale venue with an excellent restaurant is a popular gay and lesbian spot of long-standing. "Guys as Dolls" and other acts in the Crystal Room Cabaret nightly.

4 Graffiti
MAP A6 ▪ 721 Duval St, Key West
Trendy and pricey styles designed with the younger male in mind. Most of the fashions are understated, but there's also plenty of flash to suit the mood of this sybaritic island.

5 Bourbon Street Complex
MAP A6 ▪ 722 – 801 Duval St, Key West
Included here are the Bourbon Street Pub, the 801 Bourbon Bar, One Saloon, Pizza Joe's, and the New Orleans House (a gay guesthouse). 801 features nightly drag shows.

6 Gay and Lesbian Community Center
MAP A6 ▪ 513 Truman Ave, Key West ▪ 305-292-3223 ▪ www.glcckeywest.org
There's always plenty of information here for the taking, as well as occasional meetings and social events.

7 Aqua Night Club
MAP A6 ▪ 711 Duval St, Key West ▪ 305-294-0555
This vibrant club features happy hour at 3pm and a karaoke and drag show. The poolside bar out back is quieter, with torches and a waterfall.

8 Island House
MAP A6 ▪ 1129 Fleming St, Key West ▪ 305-294-6284
Acclaimed hotel and resort popular for its inviting café and bar, as well as its clothing-optional pool.

9 Santa Maria Suites
MAP A6 ▪ 1401 Simonton St, Key West ▪ 305-296-5678
Located 2.5 miles (3 km) from the airport and 8 minutes from the beach, this classy resort is popular with gay and lesbian travelers.

10 AIDS Memorial
MAP A6 ▪ Atlantic Ocean end of White Street Pier
Squares of black granite are engraved with the names of Conchs who have been taken by the disease, along with some poignant poetry.

Drag queen, Bourbon Street Complex

Bars, Pubs, and Clubs

Traditional saloon, Captain Tony's

1 Captain Tony's Saloon
MAP A6 ▪ 428 Greene St, Key West ▪ 305-294-1838

This was the original Sloppy Joe's, where Hemingway was a regular. Live bands feature; Conch hero Jimmy Buffett used to sing here.

2 Sloppy Joe's
MAP A6 ▪ 201 Duval St, Key West ▪ 305-296-2388

You can get a full meal as well as just a drink at this always noisy bar. It's heavy on Hemingway memorabilia, since he used to hang out here as well as at the original Sloppy Joe's.

3 Green Parrot Bar
MAP A6 ▪ 601 Whitehead St, Key West ▪ 305-294-6133

Hog's Breath sign

Established in 1890 and still going strong. Lots of locals, pool tables, and all kinds of live music on weekends.

4 Bull and Whistle Bar
MAP A6 ▪ 224 Duval St, Key West ▪ 305-296-4545

Three bars in one, on three different floors. Street level always has some live entertainment; the top floor deck houses the Garden of Eden (see p57), the famous clothing-optional bar.

5 Jimmy Buffet's Margaritaville
MAP A6 ▪ 500 Duval St, Key West ▪ 305-292-1435

Local-boy-made-good Jimmy Buffett is the owner of this bar-restaurant-souvenir shop. There is live music nightly, and on occasion the Parrot Head leader himself shows up.

6 The Porch
MAP A6 ▪ 429 Caroline St, Key West ▪ 305-517-6358

There is indeed a comfortable porch attached to this congenial neighborhood bar, located inside the historic Porter Mansion. Offers a varied selection of wines and craft beers.

7 Schooner Wharf Bar
MAP A6 ▪ 202 William St, Key West ▪ 305-292-3302

This bar is located in the Historic Seaport District, offering open-air views of the waterfront and live music.

8 Hog's Breath Saloon
MAP A6 ▪ 400 Front St, Key West ▪ 305-296-4222

One of the best-known bars due to a far-reaching ad campaign – it's part of a Florida chain. Expect a traditional saloon bar setting, lots of heavy drinking, and live music.

9 The Rum Bar
MAP A6 ▪ 1115 Duval St, Key West ▪ 305-296-2680

Enjoy authentic, well-made island cocktails while relaxing on the wraparound porch, with lively people-watching opportunities. Located in the Speakeasy Inn.

10 Rick's Bar/Durty Harry's Entertainment Complex
MAP A6 ▪ 202 Duval St, Key West ▪ 305-296-4890

This large complex has eight bars, and Rick's upstairs is one of the hottest dance clubs in town.

→ See map on pp120–21

Conch Dining

PRICE CATEGORIES

For a three-course meal for one with half
a bottle of wine (or equivalent meal),
taxes, and extra charges.

$ under $35 $$ $35–$70 $$$ over $70

---

1 A & B Lobster House
MAP A6 ▪ 700 Front St, Key
West ▪ 305-294-5880 ▪ $$
Maine lobster, fresh shrimp, and
waterfront views in a historic building.

2 Tavern N Town
MAP A6 ▪ 3841 N Roosevelt
Blvd, Key West ▪ 305-296-3676 ▪ $$
Floribbean cuisine is served in the
elegant surroundings of the Tavern
N Town. Try the conch chowder.

3 Blue Heaven
MAP A6 ▪ 729 Thomas St, Key
West ▪ 305-296-8688 ▪ $$
Trademark Key West chickens and
cats wander about in the garden of
this wonderful Caribbean restaurant.

4 Mangoes
MAP A6 ▪ 700 Duval St, Key
West ▪ 305-294-8002 ▪ $
Go for the exciting food (try their sig-
nature wild mushroom and truffle
"martini") but also because the place
is so central to Key West life.

5 Louie's Backyard
MAP A6 ▪ 700 Waddell
Ave, Key West ▪ 305-294-
1062 ▪ $$
Enticing haute cuisine
in a breezy, easy
setting right on
the Atlantic.

6 Michaels Restaurant
MAP A6 ▪ 532 Margaret St
and Southard, Key West ▪ 305-295-
1300 ▪ $$
For the best steak in town, head
to Michaels. Try the Cowboy steak,
a 20-oz (500-g) prime on-the-bone
rib eye with mushrooms and onions.

**7 Mangia Mangia
Pasta Café**
MAP A6 ▪ 900 Southard St, Key West
▪ 305-294-2469 ▪ $$
Open only for dinner, this central
Italian eatery has superb fresh
pasta. As a result, it's always busy.
Tasty sauces and great lasagne.

8 Sarabeth's
MAP A6 ▪ 530 Simonton St at
Southard, Key West ▪ 305-293-8181
▪ $$
The fluffy omelets, pumpkin waffles,
and lemon ricotta pancakes make
this a favorite for Sunday brunch.

9 El Siboney
MAP A6 ▪ 900 Catherine St,
Key West ▪ 305-296-4184 ▪ $
Great Cuban food in abundance in a
no-nonsense setting. Lots of diversity,
such as roast pork with cassava and
tamale, or breaded *palomilla* steak.

10 One Duval
MAP A6 ▪ Pier House Resort,
1 Duval St, Key West ▪ 305-296-4600
▪ $$
The chef utilizes the abundance
of ingredients indigenous to the
Caribbean and the Florida peninsula,
preparing them with a flourish that
redefines regional cuisine.

Spectacular views from One Duval

🔟 Side Trips

If you venture out of the more touristed confines of Greater Miami, be ready for something quite different. The Everglades look and feel competely different to the coast, especially compared to glitzy South Beach, and even the Gulf Coast and Treasure Coast enclaves seem to exist in a world apart. Gone entirely is the international feel, and in its place is a sense of the old Florida.

Naples pier with the lovely pink sunset reflecting on the water

SIDE TRIPS

The Everglades, across the Tamiami Trail (Hwy 41) 6

Sanibel and Captiva Islands

Naples and Around

A1A North along the Gold Coast 5

A1A North along the Treasure Coast

Loxahatchee National Wildlife Refuge 4

Big Cypress Siminole Reservation

The Everglades, across Alligator Alley (I-75)

Dry Tortugas from Key West 3

- **1** Top 10 Sights
  see pp133–5
- **①** Places to Eat
  see p136
- **①** Places to Stay
  see p137

1 Fort Myers
MAP A2

Although the town is historically famous as the base of operations for the 19th-century inventor Thomas Alva Edison, modern Fort Myers has become one of the main escapes for Midwesterners seeking a holiday by the sea, especially in winter. Its beaches have the feel of Indiana or Iowa about them, full of families without any of the Miami obsessions with style. The only problems you're likely to encounter are traffic snarls.

2 Sanibel and Captiva Islands
MAP A3

The Lee Island Coast has irresistible sandy beaches, exotic wildlife, lush vegetation, and wonderful sunsets. The jewels in the crown are the Sanibel and Captiva Islands, which have a Caribbean-style laid-back vibe mixed with upscale shops and restaurants. Much of the territory is protected, and development limited: there are no condos and few hotels, mainly just houses and cottages scattered among the greenery.

3 Dry Tortugas from Key West
MAP A5 ■ Yankee Freedom 305-294-7009

Travel to the wonderful islands of the Dry Tortugas by seaplane or ferry from Key West. The Yankee Freedom ferry company offers a daily trip. The day-long tours include food and snorkeling gear. Camping overnight is also possible. The most visited island is Garden Key, the site of Fort Jefferson and its fantastic snorkeling beaches *(see p55)*.

Loxahatchee National Wildlife Refuge

4 Loxahatchee National Wildlife Refuge
MAP D3 ■ 10216 Lee Rd, Boynton Beach ■ 800-683-5873
■ Open sunrise–sunset daily ■ Adm

This is the only surviving remnant of the northern Everglades, a vast area of mostly sawgrass marsh that is so characteristic of the Everglades environment. The inviting public-use areas provide viewing opportunities for a large variety of wetland flora and fauna, including egrets, alligators, and the endangered snail kite. Activities include nature walks, hiking, canoeing, bird-watching, and bass-fishing. A 5-mile (8-km) canoe trail provides the best way to see and explore the refuge up close.

5 A1A North along the Treasure Coast
MAP D2

If you continue on the A1A north of Palm Beach, the megalopolis gives way to the smaller, quieter towns of the Treasure Coast. These include Vero, the largest; Jupiter, which has no barrier islands; Stuart, with its charming historic district; rural-feeling Fort Pierce; and, at the northern extension of the Treasure Coast, the fishing village of Sebastian.

Fort Jefferson, Dry Tortugas

6 The Everglades, across the Tamiami Trail (Highway 41)
MAP A3–C4

Highway 41 was the first cut across the Everglades and from its inception has been called the Tamiami Trail, which sounds like a Native American word but stands for Tampa-Miami, the two cities it connects. However, it does take you into Seminole country, where you can experience the wonders of the Everglades *(see pp34–5)*. As you head to the Gulf Coast, stop at Everglades City and Naples.

City Hall, Everglades City

7 A1A North along the Gold Coast

Starting just at the northern tip of Miami Beach is a stretch of beautiful, wealthy communities that goes on for at least 50 miles (80 km). As diverse in their own ways as the Greater Miami area, they add immeasurably to the cultural richness of South Florida and make an unsurpassed choice for beaching it, too *(see pp30–31)*.

Beach hugging the Gold Coast road

8 Naples and Around
MAP A3

If you cross the Everglades, your inevitable first stop on the Gulf Coast will be Naples. This wealthy beach city prides itself on a manicured beauty, 55 golf courses, and an elegant downtown area. There's a pleasant pier where you can commune with pelicans or do some fishing, and 10 miles (16 km) of pristine, sugary beaches, with warmer waters than the Atlantic Ocean. Nearby Marco Island, the most northerly of the Ten Thousand Islands archipelago, is a good base for delving into the western fringe of the Everglades. It has been the source of significant Calusa Native American finds, some dating back 3,500 years.

9 Big Cypress Seminole Reservation
MAP C3 ■ Accessible from Rte 833 off the I-75

Located on the northern border of the Big Cypress National Preserve, the largest Seminole reservation in the state of Florida is the best place to meet the locals and get some sense of the lives of the modern tribe. The main Seminole settlement can be found 15 miles (24 km) north of the I-75, and has a few basic diners and gift shops, as well as the illuminating Ah-Tah-Thi-Ki Museum *(see p34)*, where videos, a rare collection of clothing and artifacts, and exhibitions by Seminole artists highlight the history and cultural traditions of the tribe.

Alligator Alley in the Everglades

⑩ The Everglades, across Alligator Alley (I-75)
MAP B3–C3

This toll road across the Everglades keeps you at arm's length from the swampy, teeming mass. There are several great stops along the way, as you pass through Big Cypress National Preserve and north of Fakahatchee Strand State Preserve (see p35).

THE SOUTH FLORIDA LAND RUSH

South Florida's warm winter climate and the economic upswing of the early 20th century made it seem a perfect place to build the American Dream. The 1920s saw the first great land boom, when prime land was $26,000 per acre and rampant development threatened to make the Everglades a memory. The bubble burst after a 1926 hurricane and the Great Depression.

A DAY TRIP ALONG THE A1A NORTH OF FORT LAUDERDALE

▶ MORNING

Drive north along **Highway A1A** (see pp30–31) to ritzy Boca Raton, one of South Florida's wealthiest communities and sprinkled with 1920s Mediterranean Revival architecture by Addison Mizner. Stop at the **Gumbo Limbo Nature Center** (see p55), and stroll its mangrove forest boardwalks to watch for ospreys, brown pelicans, and the occasional manatee. Pop across to adjacent **Red Reef Park** (see p55) for sunbathing on the beach and swimming. Retrace your route south back to the Palmetto Park Road junction and turn right – a block on the right is local favorite **Boca Beach House** (887 E Palmetto Park Rd). Have lunch here.

AFTERNOON

Continue 9 miles (14 km) north on Highway A1A to the Sandoway Discovery Center in Delray Beach. In a 1936 beachfront house, exhibits include a butterfly garden, shell gallery, and coral reef pool with live sharks. Drive 9 miles (14 km) north before taking a left at Ocean Avenue for a pit stop at the **Old Key Lime House** (p77) in Lantana, a 19th-century throwback with great Key lime pies. End the day with a final 9 miles (14 km) along the A1A to **Palm Beach** (see p76), the island town known for its palatial homes and more Mizner Mediterranean-style architecture. Take in the plush shops along **Worth Avenue** (see p30), before cocktails at the opulent **Breakers** (see p30).

See map on p132 ⬅

Places to Stay

PRICE CATEGORIES
For a standard double room per night
(with breakfast if included), taxes, and
extra charges.
....
$ under $200 $$ $200–$400 $$$ over $400

1 Billie Swamp Safari, Everglades

MAP B3 ■ Big Cypress Reservation
■ 863-983-6101 ■ www.billieswamp.
com ■ $

The amenities are little better than
camping out, but this is a chance to
get up close and personal with the
Everglades. No private baths.

2 Rod and Gun Lodge, Everglades

MAP B4 ■ 200 Riverside Dr,
Everglades City ■ 239-695-2101
■ No credit cards ■ www.
evergladesrodandgun.com ■ $

This place in the Everglades
has a colorful past that includes
stays by Hemingway, US
presidents, and Mick Jagger.

3 Hyatt Regency Pier 66, Fort Lauderdale

MAP D3 ■ 2301 SE 17th St
Causeway, Fort Lauderdale ■ 888-
591-1234 ■ www.hyatt.com ■ $$

Fantastic views from the revolving
Pier Top Lounge. Facilities include a
spa, and rooms are nicely decorated.

4 Palm Beach Hibiscus, West Palm Beach

MAP D2 ■ 213 Rosemary Ave, West
Palm Beach ■ 561-623-3308 ■ www.
palmbeachhibiscus.com ■ $

Victorian decor, exquisite china, and
individually outfitted rooms, plus an
outstanding pool and patio area.

5 Jupiter Beach Resort

MAP D2 ■ 5 North A1A, Jupiter
■ 800-228-8810 ■ www.
jupiterbeachresort.com ■ $$

The rooms are simple but have
marble baths, colorful furnishings,
and (mostly) terrific views.

6 Marriott Sanibel Harbour Resort and Spa

MAP A3 ■ 17260 Harbour Pointe Dr,
Fort Myers ■ 800-767-7777 ■ www.
marriott.com ■ $$$

Spacious and light rooms, and a
recreational area with a private beach.

7 Captiva Island Inn

MAP A3 ■ 11508 Andy Rosse
Lane, Captiva Island ■ 800-454-9898
■ www.captivaislandinn.com ■ $

A collection of wood-frame cottages,
set among tropical palms and just
steps from a faultless beach.

Suite at the Inn on Fifth

8 Inn on Fifth, Naples

MAP A3 ■ 699 5th Ave S, Naples
■ 561-368-9500 ■ www.innonfifth.com
■ $$

Cozy hotel radiating Mediterranean
charm, with lavish fountains.

9 Waterstone Resort & Marina, Boca Raton

MAP D3 ■ 999 E Camino Real, Boca
Raton ■ 561-368-9500 ■ www.
waterstoneboca.com ■ $$$

On the shores of Lake Boca, this
plush hotel offers easy access to
watersports and waterside dining.

10 Clewiston Inn

MAP C2 ■ 108 Royal Palm Ave
■ 800-749-4466 ■ www.clewistoninn.
com ■ $

This charming inn evokes a pre-Civil
War atmosphere with its decor.

See map on p132

Places to Eat

1 Chef Jean-Pierre's, Fort Lauderdale

MAP D3 ▪ 1436 N Federal Hwy ▪ 954-563-2700 ▪ $$$

This gourmet cooking school offers a real culinary experience; book meals and demonstrations online.

2 Okeechobee Steakhouse, West Palm Beach

MAP D2 ▪ 2854 Okeechobee Blvd ▪ 561-683-5151 ▪ $$$

Old-fashioned steakhouse open since 1947, knocking out juicy bone-in rib eye and porterhouse steaks, as well as a celebrated coconut cream pie.

3 The Veranda, Fort Myers

MAP A2 ▪ 2122 2nd St ▪ 239-332-2065 ▪ $$

Charming restaurant, with Deep South decor. The artichoke fritter stuffed with blue crab is outstanding.

4 Swamp Water Café

MAP C2 ▪ 30000 Gator Tail Trail ▪ 863-983-6491 ▪ $$$

The menu features classic traditional American dishes and Native American delicacies. Try the catfish, frog legs, and gator tail nuggets.

5 Joanie's Blue Crab Café, Ochopee

MAP B4 ▪ 39395 Tamiami Trail E ▪ 239-695-2682 ▪ $

An old-fashioned seafood shack on the edge of the Everglades that usually only opens at weekends.

Bikes outside Joanie's Blue Crab Café

PRICE CATEGORIES
For a three-course meal for one with half a bottle of wine (or equivalent meal), taxes, and extra charges.

$ under $35 $$ $35–$70 $$$ over $70

---

6 Rod and Gun Club, Everglades City

MAP B4 ▪ 200 Riverside Dr City ▪ 239-695-2101 ▪ No credit cards ▪ $

In a classic Florida frontier hotel, with great views and fresh fish sandwiches.

7 Sinclair's Ocean Grill, Jupiter

MAP D2 ▪ Jupiter Beach Resort, 5 North A1A ▪ 561-745-7120 ▪ $$

Traditional Floribbean food – a bit of Caribbean, Pacific Rim, and Floridian.

8 The Dock at Crayton Cove, Naples

MAP A3 ▪ 845 12th Ave S at Naples Bay ▪ 239-263-9940 ▪ $$

More Floribbean crossover cuisine, with macadamia fried goat cheese and Jamaican jerk chicken quesadilla.

9 Keylime Bistro, Captiva

MAP A3 ▪ 11509 Andy Rosse Lane ▪ 239-395-4000 ▪ $$

Fun and funky, with a beachy feel. Try the tricolor vegetarian terrine.

10 Blue Coyote Supper Club, Sanibel

MAP A3 ▪ 1100 Par View Dr ▪ 239-472-9222 ▪ $$

American fine dining at the Sanibel Island Golf Club.

Streetsmart

**Art Deco and bright colors
at Miami's South Beach**

Getting To and Around Miami and the Keys

Arriving by Air

Miami International Airport is an American Airlines' hub and primary gateway to Latin America, though most major international airlines serve Miami (including United, Delta, and Southwest, and British Airways and Virgin Atlantic from the UK).

The MIA Mover (free) links the airport with the Miami Intermodal Center, comprising the Rental Car Center and Miami Central Station (with bus services). The fastest way into the city is Metrorail's Orange Line to Coconut Grove, Wynwood, Coral Gables, or Downtown. From the bus terminal, the Miami Beach Airport Express runs directly to South Beach every 30 minutes 6am–11:40pm daily.

Taxis and **SuperShuttle** shared vans are available; both charge according to a zone system, with rates varying widely; confirm the price before starting.

Fort Lauderdale-Hollywood International Airport is the region's second airport. It's ideal if you're staying along the southern part of the Gold Coast. Broward County Transit bus No. 1 provides a cheap service to Fort Lauderdale, and there are free shuttles to the nearest Tri-Rail station at Dania Beach.

Although **Palm Beach International Airport** is much smaller, it serves many US and Canadian destinations. **Palm Tran** runs local bus services Nos. 42 and 44 into West Palm Beach, and there are free shuttles to the nearest Tri-Rail station (also at West Palm Beach).

Key West International Airport serves only a handful of US destinations with primarily American, Delta, and Silver Airways.

Arriving by Train

Amtrak serves Miami with its Silver Meteor and Silver Star lines (New York via Washington, D.C., Savannah, Orlando, and Tampa). The main station, Miami Central Station, is at the airport, with connections to local buses, taxis, and Metrorail. Amtrak trains stop at Fort Lauderdale and West Palm Beach.

Arriving by Sea

Officially "PortMiami," the **Port of Miami** is, quite simply, the largest cruise ship hub in the world. Its seven terminals are easily accessible by car or taxi, though most cruise lines docking here offer direct shuttle services to Miami International Airport, which has a variety of onward connections.

Arriving by Road

The major Interstates that lead to Miami are I-95 down the north coast, and I-75 from the Gulf Coast. There is also Florida's Turnpike, shooting down from Central Florida. These highways are well maintained, with welcome centers along the way. Highways 1, A1A, and 41 are not efficient unless you want to explore the Greater Miami area.

The main city bus station is now part of Miami Central Station near the airport, with a range of onward connections. The **Greyhound** bus is a good, although fairly slow, option for getting from Miami to Key West (four and a half hours), where the bus station is located at the airport. Greyhound also serves Fort Lauderdale, West Palm Beach, and most coastal towns in between.

Getting Around by Bus, Metro, and Train

Metrobus covers the whole Miami-Dade area. You'll need the correct change, or a stored-value EASY Card or EASY Ticket (a more limited paper ticket valid for 60 days; $2.25 a ride), available at machines at the airport, any Metrorail station, or the Transit Service Center at 111 NW First Street.

The free **Miami Beach Trolley** offers four routes running every 10–15 minutes 6am–midnight Monday–Saturday and 8am–midnight Sunday. Routes include North Beach to Normandy Isle, 41st Street to Collins Avenue (Middle Beach loop), and the South Beach Trolley loop – with stops between 5th Street and Lincoln Road. The Collins Express trolley route links the Middle Beach and North Beach trolleys.

Metrorail is a 25-mile (40-km) elevated rail system with a useful link to Miami airport. To ride the Metrorail you must use an EASY Card or EASY Ticket. It serves Downtown, Coconut Grove, and Coral Gables. Metromover is a free monorail extension of Metrorail that runs a circuit around Downtown.

For train service, there's Tri-Rail, linking Miami's Metrorail and airport with stops up and down the Gold Coast, including Fort Lauderdale, Hollywood, Delray Beach, and West Palm Beach.

Getting Around by Taxi

Miami's Yellow Cab Taxis start at $2.50 for the first sixth of a mile, and click away speedily at $2.40 a mile, so they're not a good deal for long distances. If you have a smartphone, try Uber, which is fairly safe and convenient in Miami. In Fort Lauderdale, the Fort Lauderdale Water Taxi is a fun way to explore the "Venice of America."

Getting Around by Car

All major rental agencies are represented at the state's airports and in big cities, though it's cheaper to book online in advance. You'll need a valid driver's license, photo ID, and a credit card (cash and debit cards are rarely accepted). Watch out for hidden extras. Some toll roads in Florida do not have manual payment booths; you must have a SunPass or pay "toll-by-plate" (a camera records your license plate and you're sent a bill for tolls plus a service charge). If you're renting, your company will pass the charge on to you – check the rental policy in advance.

Getting Around by Bicycle

Bikes are ideal for getting around South Beach (Miami), Key Biscayne, or Key West, but are not recommended elsewhere in Miami or South Florida, where cars dominate. DecoBike has several rental stations in Miami Beach, while BikeMan Bike Rentals offers eight locations in Key West.

DIRECTORY

ARRIVING BY AIR

Fort Lauderdale-Hollywood International Airport
℡ 954-359-1200
ⓦ fll.net

Key West International Airport
℡ 305-809-5200
ⓦ keywestinternational-airport.com

Miami International Airport
℡ 305-876-7000
ⓦ miami-airport.com

Palm Beach International Airport
℡ 561-471-7400
ⓦ pbia.org

Palm Tran
ⓦ discover.pbcgov.org/palmtran

SuperShuttle
℡ 305-871-2000
ⓦ supershuttle.com

ARRIVING BY TRAIN

Amtrak
ⓦ amtrak.com

ARRIVING BY SEA

Port of Miami
ⓦ miamidade.gov/portmiami

ARRIVING BY ROAD

Greyhound
ⓦ greyhound.com

GETTING AROUND BY BUS, METRO, AND TRAIN

Metrobus, Metromover and Metrorail
℡ 311 or 305-468-5900
ⓦ miamidade.gov/transit

Miami Beach Trolley
℡ 305-673-7117
ⓦ miamibeachfl.gov/transportation

Tri-Rail
℡ 800-874-7245
ⓦ tri-rail.com

GETTING AROUND BY TAXI

Fort Lauderdale Water Taxi
ⓦ watertaxi.com

Uber
ⓦ uber.com

Yellow Cab Taxis
ⓦ mysureride.com

GETTING AROUND BY CAR

SunPass
℡ 888-865-5352
ⓦ sunpass.com

GETTING AROUND BY BICYCLE

BikeMan Bike Rentals
ⓦ bikemanbikerental keywest.com

DecoBike
ⓦ decobike.com

Practical Information

Passports and Visas

Under the US Visa Waiver Program, visitors from Australia, New Zealand, the UK, Ireland, and most European countries do not require visas for visits shorter than 90 days. You must apply for an online **ESTA** (Electronic System for Travel Authorization), however, before you fly or arrive on a cruise ship. Do this only on the official website. There is a $4 processing fee and a $10 authorization fee once the ESTA has been approved (all paid online via credit card). In most cases it will be granted immediately, but it could take up to 72 hours. Authorizations are valid for multiple entries to the US for around two years. You'll need to present a machine-readable passport to immigration upon arrival, and fill out a customs form (one per family). Canadians will need a passport to cross the border, but can travel throughout the US for up to a year without a visa or visa waiver.

Along with other major countries, **Australia**, the **UK**, **Canada**, and **Ireland** have consular representation in Florida.

Customs and Immigration

Duty-free allowances for visitors over 21 years of age entering the US are: 1 liter (2 pints) of alcohol, gifts worth up to $100, and 200 cigarettes, 100 cigars (but not Cuban), or 3 lbs (1.4 kg) of tobacco. A number of goods are prohibited, including meat products, cheese, fresh fruit, and illegal drugs.

Travel Safety Advice

Visitors can get up-to-date travel safety information from the **UK Foreign and Commonwealth Office**, the **US Department of State**, and the **Australian Department of Foreign Affairs and Trade**.

Travel Insurance

This is essential for foreign visitors – be sure any medical coverage includes accidental death and emergency care, trip cancellation, and baggage or document loss.

Health

For the average traveler, a case of sunburn is about the most serious injury that can be sustained in Florida, although biting and stinging insects, including annoying mosquitoes, can be a real nuisance, especially between June and November.

If you do get sick or have an accident, you'll find that healthcare in Florida is excellent, but treatment and prescription drugs can get very expensive, so make sure to organize insurance before your trip. Even basic care at a hospital emergency room can potentially rise from $300 to $15,000 incredibly fast (fees for appliances, drugs, supplies, and the attendant physician are all charged separately) – only go in if you are very sick. Should you be in a serious accident, an ambulance will pick you up and charge later. Treatment for a simple leg break, for example, will total around $3,000, but if it requires surgery your final bill could range from $20,000 to $35,000.

Most South Florida hospitals, such as **Coral Gables Hospital**, **Mercy Hospital Miami**, and **Mount Sinai Medical Center**, operate 24-hour emergency rooms, and there are a number of walk-in clinics for non-emergencies, where a one-time fee of $100–$125 is usually payable (much cheaper than emergency rooms). The **Miami Urgent Care Center** is a dependable option in Miami, while **Advanced Urgent Care** is a recommended option in the Key West area.

The majority of hotels and resorts will have links to local practices, but seeing a local GP at short notice is usually very difficult for non-resident patients (unless it is considered to be an emergency). There are 24-hour drugstores such as **Walgreens** in most areas (see their website for locations and opening hours), although keep in mind that foreign prescriptions for drugs will not be honored.

Personal Security

Violent crime in Florida has dropped to historic lows since the 1990s, though Miami Beach still tends to post the highest rates in the state. At night you should be cautious wherever you are, though all the major tourist and nightlife areas are invariably brightly lit and well policed. By being careful, planning ahead, following common sense precautions, and taking good care of your possessions, you shouldn't encounter any real problems.

Car crime does remain an issue at night. When driving, under no circumstances stop in any unlit or seemingly deserted urban area, and especially not if someone is waving you down, suggesting there is something wrong with your car. Similarly, if you are "accidentally" rammed by the driver behind, do not stop immediately but drive on to the nearest well-lit, busy and secure area (such as a hotel, tollbooth,

or petrol station) and call the **emergency number** for assistance. While driving, keep your car doors locked and the windows never more than slightly open (as you'll most likely be using air-conditioning, you'll probably want to keep them fully closed anyway).

Always store your valuables in your hotel safe when you go out, and when inside keep your door locked and don't open it to anyone you don't trust; if they claim to be hotel staff and you don't believe them, call reception to check.

Travelers with Specific Needs

The US has one of the best infrastructures in the world for people with specific needs. All public buildings have to be

wheelchair-accessible and have suitable toilets, many city street corners have dropped kerbs, and most city buses are able to "kneel" to make access easier. It's unusual for any part of a hotel or motel in South Florida to be difficult for a person with mobility issues to reach, and often several bedrooms are designated "accessible." See the **Mobility International USA** and **SATH** websites for further information.

Even in rural Florida, facilities are excellent; most state parks arrange programs for visitors with specific needs (see the website of the **Florida Disabled Outdoors Association** for information). In the Everglades National Park, all walking trails are accessible, as is one of the backcountry camping sites.

DIRECTORY

PASSPORTS AND VISAS

Australia (Miami)
w usa.embassy.gov.au

Canada (Miami)
w travel.gc.ca

ESTA
w esta.cbp.dhs.gov

Ireland (Orlando)
w embassyofireland.org

UK (Miami)
w ukinusa.fco.gov.uk

TRAVEL SAFETY ADVICE

Australian Department of Foreign Affairs and Trade
w dfat.gov.au
w smartraveller.gov.au

UK Foreign and Commonwealth Office
w gov.uk/foreign-travel-advice

US Department of State
w travel.state.gov

HEALTH

Advanced Urgent Care
1980 N Roosevelt Blvd, Key West
c 305-294-0011
w urgentcarefloridakeys.com

Coral Gables Hospital
3100 Douglas Rd, Coral Gables
c 305-445-8461
w coralgableshospital.com

Mercy Hospital Miami
3663 S Miami Ave, Coconut Grove
c 305-854-4400
w mercymiami.com

Miami Urgent Care Center
2645 Douglas Rd
c 305-494-0536
w miamiurgentcare.com

Mount Sinai Medical Center
4300 Alton Rd, Miami Beach
c 305-574-2273
w msmc.com

Walgreens
w walgreens.com

PERSONAL SECURITY

Emergency Number
c 911

TRAVELERS WITH SPECIFIC NEEDS

Florida Disabled Outdoors Association
w fdoa.org

Mobility International USA
w miusa.org

SATH
w sath.org

Currency and Banking

The currency is the US dollar ($), made up of 100 cents (¢). Bills (notes) come in denominations of $1, $5, $10, $20, $50, and $100, while coins are 1¢ (usually called a penny), 5¢ (nickel), 10¢ (dime), 25¢ cents (quarter) and, rarely, 50¢ (half-dollar), and one dollar.

Most people holidaying here withdraw cash as needed from ATMs, available at all bank branches, at many convenience stores, and at some delis in the city, although most charge fees of up to $3 (in addition to your home bank charges). American Express, MasterCard, and Visa credit cards are widely accepted, and are almost always required for deposits at hotels and car rental desks. Traveler's checks can occasionally be useful, but these days they are outdated and almost pointless.

Most banks are open 8:30am–5pm Monday–Friday, and a few have limited Saturday hours.

Note that unlike most countries, sales tax is not included in the marked price of anything in the US, including restaurant meals. Florida's sales tax at present is 6 percent, but local taxes can bump that up to 8 percent. Hoteliers in Miami Beach will generally add tax of 14 percent to your bill.

Telephone and Internet

International visitors who want to use their cell phones in Miami and the Keys will need to check with their phone provider to make sure it will work, and what the call charges will be. Unless you have a tri-band mobile, it is unlikely that a device bought for use outside the US or Canada will work inside the States (iPhones should be fine).

Even if your phone does work you'll need to be particularly careful about the roaming charges, especially for data, which can be extortionate; even checking voicemail can result in hefty charges. To avoid this, many travelers turn off voicemail and data roaming before they travel. If you have a compatible (and unlocked) GSM phone and intend to use it a lot, it can be much cheaper to buy a US SIM card ($10 or less) to use during your stay (you can also buy micro-SIMs or nano-SIMs). Some networks also sell basic flip phones (with free minutes) for as little as $25 (no paperwork or ID is required). One of the largest mobile networks is **AT&T**, which is a useful source for renting a cell phone or purchasing a SIM card.

Public telephones are becoming harder to find due to the popularity of cell phones; you'll find a few at some gas stations, restaurants, and hotels; and on the sidewalk. For making any call in Miami, even next door, you must dial the 305 area code, but not the 1 before it. The **Directory Assistance** is a useful service for finding telephone numbers.

Wireless internet is now king in Miami: a **Free WiFi Miami Beach** system for residents and visitors alike is offered. Most hotels, hostels, and coffee shops offer Wi-Fi, and there are several Wi-Fi hotspots scattered throughout the city.

A good alternative is to stop by the **Miami Beach Regional Library**, or a branch of any other public library, which will usually offer computer terminals (and free Wi-Fi) for use (although you might have to get a temporary membership first).

Postal Services

Post offices are usually open 9am–5pm on weekdays, with some open 9am–noon or later on Saturday. The most comprehensive ones are **Miami Beach Post Office** on Washington Avenue and **Key West Post Office** on Whitehead Street. Stamps are sold in many drugstores, hotels, and grocery stores. All US domestic mail goes first class, and you should use airmail for any overseas mail. Rates are currently $1.15 for letters and postcards to all international destinations (including those to Canada).

Television and Radio

Most hotel rooms in Miami and the Keys will have a TV offering access to the usual line-up of US cable channels. The programming of the main national networks are carried by four Miami channels: Channel 4 is **CBS**, Channel 6 is **NBC**, Channel 7 is **Fox**, and Channel 10 is **ABC**. Most of South Florida's radio stations stick to the usual commercial format of retro-rock, classic pop, country, or easy-listening, as well as **NPR** (National Public Radio) programming and similar local stations for people who want to hear the topics of the day. There are, of course, several Spanish-language stations.

Newspapers and Magazines

The daily *Miami Herald* is one of the most read newspapers in Florida, and its weekly supplements are major sources of information about local entertainment and events. *El Nuevo Herald* is the Spanish-language edition, which focuses more on issues and events relating to the huge Hispanic community. The *Miami New Times* is the main free alternative weekly, which you can pick up every Thursday in stores, restaurants, clubs, and drop bins all over town. It reviews restaurants, movies, clubs, and more. Fort Lauderdale's daily *South Florida Sun-Sentinel* covers South Florida, while the smaller daily *Palm Beach Post* serves Palm Beach and the Treasure Coast. The *Key West Citizen* is the only daily newspaper that is published in the Florida Keys, and features news about upcoming events, arts, theater, attractions, music, clubs, local news, features, and opinions.

Opening Hours

The majority of shops are open 9am–6pm Monday–Saturday and noon–6pm Sunday, but be aware that times can differ considerably between cities and rural areas. Most museums and tourist sights in South Florida and Miami are open daily, although they may close on either Monday or Tuesday.

Time Difference

Miami and the Keys are in the Eastern Time Zone, five hours behind Greenwich Mean Time and three hours ahead of California.

Electrical Appliances

US voltage is 110–115 volts, and electrical plugs have two flat prongs. Unless they're dual voltage (most cell phones, cameras, MP3 players, and laptops are now), all Australian, British, Irish, European, and New Zealand appliances will require a voltage transformer as well as a plug adapter (older hair-dryers are the most common problem for travelers).

DIRECTORY

TELEPHONE AND INTERNET

AT&T
1601 Washington Ave, South Beach
Open 9am–8pm Mon–Sat, 10am–6pm Sun
📞 305-674-4994
🌐 att.com

Directory Assistance
📞 411

Free WiFi Miami Beach
🌐 miamibeachfl.gov/wifi

Miami Beach Regional Library
227 22nd St, Miami Beach
Open 10am–6pm Fri–Sun, 10am–8pm Mon–Thu
📞 305-535-4219
🌐 mdpls.org

POSTAL SERVICES

Key West Post Office
400 Whitehead St
Open 8:30am–5pm Mon–Fri, 9:30am–noon Sat
📞 305-294-9539
🌐 usps.com

Miami Beach Post Office
1300 Washington Ave
Open 8am–5pm Mon–Fri, 8:30am–2pm Sat
📞 305-672-2447
🌐 usps.com

TELEVISION AND RADIO

ABC
🌐 local10.com

CBS
🌐 miami.cbslocal.com

Fox
🌐 wsvn.com

NBC
🌐 nbcmiami.com

NPR
🌐 npr.org

NEWSPAPERS AND MAGAZINES

El Nuevo Herald
🌐 elnuevoherald.com

Key West Citizen
🌐 keysnews.com

Miami Herald
🌐 miamiherald.com

Miami New Times
🌐 miaminewtimes.com

Palm Beach Post
🌐 palmbeachpost.com

South Florida Sun-Sentinel
🌐 sun-sentinel.com

Weather

South Florida, with its subtropical climate, is a year-round destination. However, late spring and summer can be uncomfortably hot, with rain almost every afternoon. The high season is from about December to April.

Roughly one in ten of the hurricanes to occur in the North Atlantic hits Florida. The hurricane season runs from June through November, with the greatest threat of storms being from August through October.

Sources of Information

The **Greater Miami CVB** (Convention and Visitors Bureau) runs both local and international offices, and a website. It offers maps and pointers on everything in the Greater Miami area, including the Keys and the Everglades. The **Miami Beach**, **Coral Gables**, **Coconut Grove**, **Fort Lauderdale**, **Key West**, and **Palm Beach Chambers of Commerce** offer information and a variety of maps.

The Miami Design Preservation League in South Beach runs the **Art Deco Welcome Center** *(see p15)*, offering guided tours as well as literature on the District and Art Deco style.

Over in Florida City, the **Tropical Everglades Visitor Association** offers tips on tours and walks, fishing and boating, diving and snorkeling.

The **Greater Fort Lauderdale CVB** offers travelers information about Fort Lauderdale,

Hollywood, and the neighboring beach towns, while the **Palm Beach CVB** covers Boca Raton, West Palm Beach, and the Treasure Coast.

Those at the **Monroe County Tourist Development Council** (the Florida Keys and Key West) know everything about the archipelago. They provide the best maps and top tips for getting the most out of every single mile marker along the way. For general tips, the **Visit Florida** website is worth a visit.

Shopping

Miami has become a major shopping hub, with everything on offer from high-end malls, to artsy galleries and indie stores.

South Beach has the most eclectic collection of shops, along Collins (see p69) and Washington (see p13) avenues and Lincoln Road Mall (see p82). Coral Gables has spruced up the offerings along its Miracle Mile (see p108), also known as SW 22nd Street, while the exclusive Bal Harbour Shops (see p68) is crammed with outrageously expensive designer stores.

The Design District (see p100) can be an intriguing area for a stroll, although it is obvious that the main emphasis is on designer furniture and art galleries, with little else on offer.

In Coconut Grove, the open-air CocoWalk (see *p107)* is still full to the brim with restaurants, bars, and a movie theater.

Miami has a growing reputation for its talented young fashion designers, which are showcased

along with the best Latin American talent at the annual Miami Fashion Week, usually held in March in South Beach.

Whatever you're in the market for, from tickets and trinkets to clothes and accessories, do a little research and price comparison. The chances are you will discover the same or similar item for less if you shop around.

Dining

Miami's cosmopolitan character is best displayed in its food, which blends the flavors of Haiti, Cuba, and the US.

The 1990s saw the development of a hybrid style of cooking known as New Floridian (also called Floribbean), which combines nouvelle cuisine methods and presentation with ingredients from the Caribbean, such as tropical fruit and fish. In the last few years this has been complemented by a wider fusion cuisine movement, which blends these styles with just about anything: Chinese, Indian, Italian, and South American. Seafood, every bit as plentiful and good as would be expected so close to fish-laden tropical waters, is a common feature on every menu. Stone-crab claws is a regional specialty, and Cuban food is a staple.

In the Keys, most menus, not surprisingly, feature fresh seafood, and you should try to sample Key lime pie and conch fritters – both Key West specialties – at least once.

Always check your bill when you get it, especially around the South Beach tourist drags, and don't forget that a 15 percent gratuity is often automatically added, which you can cross off if you're not happy with the service. Otherwise, you shouldn't depart a bar or restaurant without leaving a tip of at least 15–20 percent, unless the service is awful. If you're just drinking at a bar, a tip of $1 per drink is normal (leave it on the bar).

Accommodations

The accommodation options in Miami and the Keys range from youth hostels and the chain hotels and motels lining almost every highway to plush resorts.

Airbnb is very useful for locating unique places to stay. **Couchsurfing**, which allows travelers to book to stay with a family for a short period, can also be a fun and interesting alternative option.

The accommodation price range is vast. Even on South Beach in high season, just two blocks from the beach, you can find a room for two, with private bath, for as little as $50 per person per night. A block away, however, a penthouse suite in some fabulous Deco landmark can be as much as $2,500.

Be aware that many hotels have a minimum stay requirement, but often offer a good deal if you book by the week. If you want to go for the bargain accommodations in high season, it's crucial that you book as early as possible. Make sure the reservation is solid by guaranteeing it with a credit card, and doubly confirming it by email. If you're expecting to arrive late, find out the latest acceptable arrival time before your reservation is subject to cancellation.

Trying to find something on the spot between December to April is not recommended, at least not in South Beach or Key West, especially on weekends. It might take a long time to find, and you run the risk of having to pay even more than top dollar. Taking your chances without a reservation is only a good idea in the low season.

There can be many hidden extras added on to the bill, such as valet parking, phone calls made from your room, or hefty hotel taxes, so get it clear from the start.

Family travel is the bread-and-butter of South Florida tourism, and usually children under a certain age can stay in their parents' room at no extra charge.

DIRECTORY

Places to Stay

PRICE CATEGORIES

For a standard, double room per night (with breakfast if included), taxes, and extra charges.

$ under $200 $$ $200–$400 $$$ over $400

Luxury

EAST Miami

MAP N3 ▪ 788 Brickell Plaza, Downtown Miami ▪ 305-712-7000 ▪ www.east-miami.com ▪ $$

Plush hotel featuring rooms with a sleek Asian style and floor-to-ceiling windows. Home to the hip Uruguayan restaurant Quinto La Huella.

InterContinental Miami

MAP P2 ▪ 100 Chopin Plaza, at Biscayne Blvd ▪ 305-577-1000 ▪ www.icmiamihotel.com ▪ $$

Downtown's finest, with amazing views and fine dining. A Henry Moore sculpture adorns the lobby; the lovely rooms sport marble bathrooms.

Loews Miami Beach

MAP S3 ▪ 1601 Collins Ave, South Beach ▪ 305-604-1601 ▪ www.loewshotels.com/miami-beach ▪ $$

SoBe's biggest Deco tower is on a sandy beach. The property incorporates an outpost of New York's Lure Fishbar restaurant, an Exhale spa, and a stunning pool area.

Mayfair Hotel & Spa

MAP G3 ▪ 3000 Florida Ave, Coconut Grove ▪ 800-433-4555 ▪ www.mayfairhotelandspa.com ▪ $$

Located on the top of a shopping mall, this hotel hosts large suites with mahogany furniture, marble baths, and spacious balconies. The style is a mix of Spain and the Far East, with Art Nouveau touches.

The Ritz-Carlton, Fort Lauderdale

MAP D3 ▪ 1 North Fort Lauderdale Beach Blvd, Fort Lauderdale ▪ 954-465-2300 ▪ www.ritzcarlton.com ▪ $$

Overlooking the beach, this luxury hotel features a world-class restaurant, spa, heated infinity pool, and a state-of-the-art fitness center. It is also on the trolley line, which provides free transportation to Las Olas and other attractions.

1 Hotel South Beach

MAP S3 ▪ 2341 Collins Ave ▪ 305-604-1000 ▪ www.1hotels.com ▪ $$$

The first outpost of this exclusive hotel chain opened in South Beach in 2015, blending luxurious accommodation with eco-conscious living. LED lights, reclaimed materials and recycled wood keys are used throughout.

Biltmore Hotel

MAP F3 ▪ 1200 Anastasia Ave, Coral Gables ▪ 855-311-6903 ▪ www.biltmorehotel.com ▪ $$$

A beautiful landmark (see p24), exuding the glamour of a bygone era and epicurean delights in the Palme d'Or restaurant (see p67). Rooms are set up in the grand European hotel tradition, and it has one of the world's largest hotel pools.

The Breakers

MAP D2 ▪ 1 South County Rd, Palm Beach ▪ 877-724-3188 ▪ www.thebreakers.com ▪ $$$

A Palm Beach landmark of the Gilded-Age tradition, whose decor evokes the Spanish Revival taste that Flagler brought to Florida in the 1890s.

Four Seasons Resort, Palm Beach

MAP D2 ▪ 2800 South Ocean Blvd, Palm Beach ▪ 561-582-2800 ▪ www.fourseasons.com ▪ $$$

The service here is first-class, from fresh fruit and orchids in your large room with sea view, to a town-car shuttle to and from downtown Palm Beach, and one of the best restaurants around.

Key West Marriott Beachside

MAP A6 ▪ 3841 Roosevelt Blvd, Key West ▪ 305-296-8100 ▪ www.beachsidekeywest.com ▪ $$$

This houses the justifiably popular Tavern N Town restaurant (see p131), and offers spacious rooms, a swimming pool, and a private beach.

Mandarin Oriental Miami

MAP P3 ▪ 500 Brickell Key Dr ▪ 305-913-8288 ▪ www.mandarinoriental.com ▪ $$$

Located on Brickell Key (Claughton Island), near the Port of Miami.

The curved building means most rooms have an ocean view. Check the website for special rates.

W Miami

MAP N3 ▪ 485 Brickell Ave, Downtown Miami ▪ 305-503-4400 ▪ www. wmiamihotel.com ▪ $$$
Much of this unique hotel was designed by Kelly Wearstler, though some amenities, such as the huge pool, are the work of Philippe Starck. Enjoy sophisticated modern cuisine at the hotel's 15th & Vine restaurant.

Art Deco Hotels

The Stiles Hotel

MAP S4 ▪ 1120 Collins Ave ▪ 877-538-9299 ▪ www.thestileshotel. com ▪ $
An Art Deco edifice built in 1938 that has been impeccably restored with every comfort in mind. Modern rooms are decorated with neutral shades and natural fibers, creating a tranquil atmosphere. In-room spa treatments are available.

Washington Park Hotel

MAP R4 ▪ 1050 Washington Ave ▪ 305-421-6265 ▪ www.wph southbeach.com ▪ $
Four stunningly restored 1930s Art Deco sugar cubes are spread over the entire block between 10th and 11th streets, set amid spacious gardens.

Albion

MAP S2 ▪ 1650 James Ave at Lincoln Rd ▪ 305-913-1000 ▪ www.rubell hotels.com ▪ $$
This hotel is excellent value, considering the extreme chic that exudes from the cutting-edge restoration of this great Deco original. Be sure to check out the pool's peek-a-boo portholes.

Avalon

MAP S4 ▪ 700 Ocean Drive ▪ 305-538-0133 ▪ www. avalonhotel.com ▪ $$
Actually two hotels on opposite corners of 7th Street, these perfectly located Deco bon-bons are great value. Located in the middle of SoBe's most popular stretch, it offers comfortable rooms and a complimentary continental breakfast.

COMO Metropolitan Miami Beach

MAP S1 ▪ 2445 Collins Ave ▪ 305-695-3600 ▪ www.comohotels.com ▪ $$
A modernized Art Deco gem (it opened in 1939 as the Traymore Hotel), with light-filled rooms and interiors by Italian designer Paola Navone. Think all-white furnishings, pastel pink and pale green walls, and speckled marble floors.

Delano South Beach

MAP S2 ▪ 1685 Collins Ave ▪ 305-672-2000 ▪ www.morganshotel group.com ▪ $$
This ultra-luxurious Postmodern wonder is a SoBe gem. The original, rather austere white exterior gives way to the divine madness of Philippe Starck inside, along with hilarious Dali- and Gaudi-inspired designs. The very chi-chi Leynia restaurant is an Argentinean grill that is inspired by the flavors from Japan.

Essex House

MAP S4 ▪ 1001 Collins Ave ▪ 305-534-2700 ▪ www. clevelander.com ▪ $$
Set near SoBe's nightclubs, the Essex offers classic Art Deco luxury and detail. Guests aged 21 years and over have access to the pool and patio at the Clevelander, its sister property, next door. Free continental breakfast is included.

The Hotel of South Beach

MAP R4 ▪ 801 Collins Ave ▪ 305-531-2222 ▪ www. thehotelofsouthbeach. com ▪ $$
"Tiffany," as proclaimed by the neon tower, was this hotel's name – until the jewelry company sued. Comfortable and stylish, its interiors are the work of fashion designer Todd Oldham, The Hotel qualifies as a SoBe work of art in itself.

Hotel Victor

MAP S4 ▪ 1144 Ocean Drive ▪ 305-908-1462 ▪ www.hotelvictorsouth beach.com ▪ $$
Given a comprehensive makeover by designers Yabu Pushelberg, the Victor's original 1936 Art Deco features – elegant mosaics and a tropical mural by artist Earl LePan – are offset by designer furniture and a tank full of live jellyfish.

National Hotel

MAP S2 ▪ 1677 Collins Ave ▪ 305-532-2311 ▪ www. nationalhotel.com ▪ $$
This Art Deco hotel is one of the coolest places to see or be seen on South Beach. It also boasts one of the longest swimming pools in Florida.

Raleigh Miami Beach

MAP S2 ■ 1775 Collins Ave ■ 305-534-6300 ■ www.raleighhotel.com ■ $$
This is nothing less than fabulous, with decor that has endless style and panache, often with period pieces. The eye-popping swimming pool is immortalized in several Esther Williams movies.

Casa Grande Suite Hotel

MAP S4 ■ 834 Ocean Drive ■ 305-672-7003 ■ www.casagrandesuitehotel.com ■ $$$
This luxurious small hotel is one of the finest in the trendy South Beach area; just step right out into all the nightlife. The suites have kitchens.

Resorts and Spas

Boca Raton Resort and Club

MAP D3 ■ 501 East Camino Real, Boca Raton ■ 888-543-1277 ■ www.bocaresort.com ■ $$
Built by one of Florida's early visionaries, Addison Mizner, in 1926. A mix of Mediterranean styles and fabled luxury is everywhere, right down to the marble bathrooms with original brass fittings.

Cheeca Lodge and Spa

MAP C5 ■ 81801 Overseas Highway, Islamorada ■ 844-993-9713 ■ www.cheeca.com ■ $$
A tropical island world with a wonderful beach, various pools, golf, tennis, nature walks, hot-tubbing, sport fishing, snorkeling, windsurfing, etc.

Fontainebleau, Miami Beach

MAP H3 ■ 4441 Collins Ave ■ 800-548-8886 ■ www.fontainebleau.com ■ $$
Built in the 1950s, this is one of the great Miami Beach hotels. Rooms are large, many with amazing views, and there is a luxury pool complex and a huge beachside spa.

Hawks Cay Resort

MAP B6 ■ 61 Hawks Cay Blvd, Duck Key ■ 305-743-7000 ■ www.hawkscay.com ■ $$
An exclusive Keys resort that offers fishing, dolphin encounters, an offshore sailing school, scuba diving, snorkeling, parasailing, kayaking, water-skiing, glass-bottom boat tours, and several other exciting activities.

Carillon Miami

MAP H2 ■ 6801 Collins Ave, Miami Beach ■ 866-800-3858 ■ www.carillonhotel.com ■ $$$
Located on its own long stretch of beach, this deluxe spa and wellness resort features one- and two-bedroom suites with floor-to-ceiling windows and sensational city or ocean views.

Casa Marina, Waldorf Astoria Resort

MAP A6 ■ 1500 Reynolds St, Key West ■ 888-303-5719 ■ www.casamarinaresort.com ■ $$$
The first grand hotel in Key West still shows its posh roots. There is an air of reverie that contrasts with the pace on the rest of the hectic island. Lavish public areas lead to understated rooms, many with water views.

Fisher Island Club

MAP H3 ■ 1 Fisher Island Dr, Fisher Island ■ 305-535-6000 ■ www.fisherislandclub.com ■ $$$
The billionaires who favor this remote private island love the exclusivity that it provides. Personal golf-carts let you toodle around the beaches, restaurants, clubs, etc. A free car ferry runs every 15 minutes, off the MacArthur Causeway.

The Ritz Carlton, Key Biscayne

MAP H4 ■ 455 Grand Bay Drive, Key Biscayne ■ 305-365-4500 ■ www.ritzcarlton.com ■ $$$
Located in an exclusive area, this is a grand hotel in every respect. Beautiful interiors, two swimming pools, tennis courts, and a spa, and one of its restaurants is rated in the country's top 25.

St. Regis Bal Harbour Resort

MAP H2 ■ 9703 Collins Ave, Bal Harbour ■ 305-993-3300 ■ www.stregisbalharbour.com ■ $$$
Famed for its butler service, this lavish ocean-front property features two tropical pools, the Remède Spa, Greek restaurant Atlantikós, and access to a gorgeous white sand beach.

Trump International Beach Resort

MAP H3 ■ 18001 Collins Ave, Sunny Isles ■ 305-692-5600 ■ www.trumpmiami.com ■ $$$
Right on the ocean, this 32-floor, lushly landscaped hotel has many amenities, including a spa, a host of programs for kids, a 24-hour exercise facility, and a business center.

Trump National Doral Miami

MAP F3 ■ 4400 NW 87th Ave ■ 800-713-6725 ■ www.trumphotels.com/miami ■ $$$

Internationally famous for its championship golf course. In fact, there are seven courses, along with 15 tennis courts, a water park, health club, and a world-class spa.

Turnberry Isle Miami

MAP H1 ■ 19999 W Country Club Dr, Aventura ■ 305-932-6200 ■ www.turnberryislemiami.com ■ $$$

Very grand, with oriental carpets, marble, and acres of landscaped islands that encompass waterways, a golf course, tennis courts, private beach, and harbor. The feeling is welcoming, clubby, and very rich.

Guesthouses

Bars B&B South Beach

MAP Q4 ■ 711 Lenox Ave, South Beach ■ 305-534- 3010 ■ www.barsbandbmiami.com ■ $

Stylish B&B a few blocks from the beach. The chic, modern rooms are in minimalist greys and whites, with splashes of color from contemporary artworks. Complimentary wine and cheese nightly.

Hotel St. Michel

MAP G3 ■ 162 Alcazar Ave, at Ponce de Leon Blvd, Coral Gables ■ 800-848-4683 ■ www.hotelstmichel.com ■ $

European-style inn built in 1926, during the Merrick heyday (see p25). Each room is unique, accented by beautiful antiques.

Kaskades South Beach

MAP S2 ■ 300 17th St, South Beach ■ 844-874-4253 ■ www.kaskadeshotel.com ■ $

Right in the heart of SoBe action, this luxury inn has rooms that feature loads of plush extras for a fraction of the cost at larger hotels, such as marble wet rooms, steam enclave rain showers, and coffee makers by Nespresso.

Sea Spray Inn

MAP D3 ■ 4301 El Mar Dr, Lauderdale-By-The-Sea ■ 954-776-1311 ■ www.seasprayinn.com ■ $

This charming inn is tucked away in a small resort town 11 miles (18 km) north of Fort Lauderdale airport, steps from the beach. Each of the 16 apartments offers a fully-equipped kitchen and modern bathroom with a walk-in shower.

South Beach Hotel

MAP S2 ■ 236 21st St, South Beach ■ 305-531-3464 ■ www.southbeachhotel.com ■ $

Fully restored historic Art Deco property, in a quiet neighborhood in the northern end of SoBe. The contemporary rooms are superb value, with chic art and furnishings.

Villa Paradiso Hotel

MAP S3 ■ 1415 Collins Ave, South Beach ■ 305-532-0616 ■ www.villaparadisohotel.com ■ $

All rooms have French doors that open onto the sunny courtyard and garden, and are decorated with appealing upholstered wrought-iron furniture. Each accommodation has a full kitchen.

Deer Run Bed & Breakfast

MAP B6 ■ 1997 Long Beach Rd, Big Pine Key ■ 305-872-2015 ■ www.deerrunfloridabb.com ■ $$

Among palm trees on a white sandy beach, this is an ecofriendly Caribbean-style home where leisurely breezes and seclusion prevail. Breakfast is served overlooking the ocean.

The Gardens Hotel Key West

MAP A6 ■ 526 Angela St, Key West ■ 800-526-2664 ■ www.gardenshotel.com ■ $$

This plantation-style property is Key West's grande dame among guesthouses. Multiple buildings comprise the hotel, including Bahamian "eyebrow" cottages. All rooms have garden views and most have Jacuzzis.

Grandview Gardens

MAP D2 ■ 1608 Lake Ave, West Palm Beach ■ 561-833-9023 ■ www.grandview-gardens.com ■ $$

On a quiet block amid tropical gardens, the renovated 1925 property features gorgeous Spanish Mediterranean architecture, an enticing outdoor pool, and lavishly decorated period rooms.

Marquesa Hotel

MAP A6 ■ 600 Fleming St, Key West ■ 800-869-4631 ■ www.marquesa.com ■ $$

Constructed in 1884, the extravagant compound of four exquisitely restored Conch houses is now set amid lush greenery. All rooms and suites have marble bathrooms.

For a key to hotel price categories see p148

Mermaid & the Alligator

MAP A6 ▪ 729 Truman Ave, Key West ▪ 305-294-1894 ▪ www.kwmermaid.com ▪ $$

One of Key West's finest, a 1904 beauty with colonial Caribbean decor and wonderful gardens. Rooms are eclectic, and feel private and cozy. Full breakfast is served by the pool.

South Beach Plaza Villas

MAP S3 ▪ 1411 Collins Ave, South Beach ▪ 305-531-1331 ▪ www.southbeachplazavillas.com ▪ $$

Super-friendly and very laid-back, the place feels more like it's in the islands somewhere remote, yet you're just a block away from SoBe. The rooms have character, and there's a garden to relax in.

LGBT+ Hotels

The Grand Resort

MAP D3 ▪ 539 North Birch Rd, Fort Lauderdale ▪ 800-818-1211 ▪ www.grandresort.net ▪ $

Exclusive resort for gay men only, just steps from the beach, with simple but comfy rooms. Boasts its own full-service day spa and hair studio, offering everything from a Swedish massage to a haircut.

Hôtel Gaythering

MAP Q2 ▪ 1409 Lincoln Rd, South Beach ▪ 786-284-1176 ▪ www.gaythering.com ▪ $

Ultrastylish and wildly popular hotel that offers teeny "crate shared rooms" (that come with sound machines), and larger king rooms decorated in a playful style. Extras include Miami Beach's only gay sauna and a stylish cocktail lounge.

Hotel St. Augustine

MAP R5 ▪ 347 Washington Ave, Miami Beach ▪ 305-532-0570 ▪ www.hotelstaugustine.com ▪ $

This chic boutique hotel is stylish and LGBT-friendly. Its 24 loft-style rooms are furnished in maple wood, with ensuite bathrooms featuring spa-like steam showers.

Island House South Beach

MAP S3 ▪ 1428 Collins Ave, South Beach ▪ 800-382-2422 ▪ www.islandhousesouthbeach.com ▪ $

This charming restored Art Deco property is in the heart of South Beach. Basic furnishings, casual atmosphere, and a variety of rooms are available at reasonable rates; some have shared bathrooms.

Royal Palms Resort

MAP D3 ▪ 717 Breakers Ave, Fort Lauderdale ▪ 954-565-5790 ▪ www.royalpalms.com ▪ $

Gay men only are catered to at this resort, which features three swimming pools, a poolside café, an on-site spa and a fitness center, all set in lush tropical surroundings.

Alexander's Guesthouse

MAP A6 ▪ 1118 Fleming St, Key West ▪ 305-294-9919 ▪ www.alexanderskeywest.com ▪ $$

This carefully restored Conch-house offers 17 comfortable guest rooms, a swimming pool and a Jacuzzi, and a taste of tropical elegance. Breakfast is served poolside, and happy hour runs from 4:30 to 5:30pm.

Equator Resort

MAP A6 ▪ 822 Fleming St, Key West ▪ 305-294-7775 ▪ www.equatorresort.com ▪ $$

Clothing-optional men's resort in the core of Key West's primary gay district on historic Fleming Street. The resort's rooms are spacious and feature welcoming amenities.

Island House

MAP A6 ▪ 1129 Fleming St, Key West ▪ 800-890-6284 ▪ www.islandhousekeywest.com ▪ $$

For gay men only, this beautiful property is clothing-optional and very cruisy, featuring a poolside café, sauna, steam room, bar, and gym.

Pineapple Point Guesthouse & Resort

MAP D3 ▪ 315 NE 16th Terrace, Fort Lauderdale ▪ 888-844-7295 ▪ www.pineapplepoint.com ▪ $$

Fort Lauderdale's premier accommodation for gay men is like a tropical rain forest, with orchids and a clothing-optional pool. Every comfort has been seen to here.

Sobe You

MAP R4 ▪ 1018 Jefferson Ave at 10th St, South Beach ▪ 305-534-5347 ▪ www.sobeyou.us ▪ $$

Located in a quiet neighborhood, five blocks from the beach, this fine guesthouse offers comfortable accommodations and friendly, attentive service. Attractions include a sun deck, saltwater pool, wine-and-cheese parties, and gourmet breakfasts served by the pool.

Budget

The Chocolate Hostel
MAP D3 ▪ 506 SE 16th St, Fort Lauderdale ▪ 954-522-6350 ▪ www.hostel fortlauderdale.com ▪ $
Dorm rooms overlooking either the pool or the garden are $37 per night. This hostel is a short walk from all the amenities of Fort Lauderdale and a mile from the beach. Free Wi-Fi and parking.

The Clay
MAP S3 ▪ 1438 Washington Ave, South Beach ▪ 305-779-0461 ▪ www.clayhotel.com ▪ $
This is an enchanting Spanish-style place, built in 1925. The biggest bargain in the Western world, the Clay is always teeming with international youth. Ensure you book very far in advance.

Everglades International Hostel
MAP E6 ▪ 20 SW 2nd Ave, Florida City ▪ 305-248-1122 ▪ www.everglades hostel.com ▪ $
The incredible amenities include whimsical tropical gardens, free internet access, free calls to anywhere in the US, a large-screen movie room, laundry facilities, a fully equipped kitchen, and free pancakes.

Hollywood Beach Suites & Hotel
MAP D3 ▪ 344 Arizona St, Hollywood ▪ 954-391-9448 ▪ www.hollywood-beachsuitehotel.com ▪ $
The cheapest rooms here (designed for families or large groups) are a great deal, with sleek, modern furnishings, two bunks and space for up to six people. The property is just steps from the beach, where you can eat at the on-site Taco Beach Shack.

Miami Beach International Hostel
MAP R4 ▪ 236 9th St, South Beach ▪ 305-534-0268 ▪ www.hostel miamibeach.com ▪ $
This is a very social South Beach hostel that attracts a youthful, international crowd thanks to its lively freebies, which include DJs spinning discs, live music, streetside patio, games, and more. Rooms range from dorms for six to singles with private en suite. Expect a fun but noisy experience.

Miami Hostel
MAP Q4 ▪ 810 Alton Road, Miami Beach ▪ 305-538-7030 ▪ www. miamihostel.net ▪ $
This friendly hostel guarantees a fun-filled stay. Excellent facilities include a Jacuzzi and pool table, and organized tours can be arranged, including a bar crawl. Breakfast and Wi-Fi are included in the price.

Ocean Blue Hostel
MAP S4 ▪ 928 Ocean Drive, Miami Beach ▪ 305-763-8212 ▪ www. oceanblue.miami ▪ $
This newly renovated hostel in the heart of the Art Deco District offers only dorm rooms. Free breakfast, Wi-Fi, and rooftop parties make it an affordable and lively option. Some rooms have oceanfront views and en suite bathrooms.

Posh South Beach Hostel
MAP R4 ▪ 820 Collins Ave, Miami Beach ▪ 305-674-8821 ▪ www.poshsouth beach.com ▪ $
As the name suggests, this is a "luxurious 5-star boutique" hostel, which in practice means designer bunk beds, plasma TVs, free fitness classes, airport shuttle, and free-drink happy hours.

Seashell Motel & Key West Hostel
MAP A6 ▪ 718 South St, Key West ▪ 305-296-5719 ▪ www.keywesthostel. com ▪ $
Offers snorkeling trips and scuba instruction, plus bike rentals. It has a courtyard, picnic area, and game rooms, but only ten private rooms, so book in advance.

SoBe Hostel & Bar
MAP R5 ▪ 235 Washington Ave, South Beach ▪ 305-534-6669 ▪ www.sobe-hostel.com ▪ $
This is the southernmost hostel on South Beach, located in the heart of the Art Deco District. Free breakfast and transfers to the airport are included, along with a full bar until 5am and an internet café.

Tropics Hotel and Hostel
MAP S3 ▪ 1550 Collins Ave, South Beach ▪ 305-531-0362 ▪ www.tropics hotel.com ▪ $
This is a genuine Art Deco building, complete with neon marquee, in a desirable location on South Beach. It's clean and comfortable and, given the location, worth two to three times the asking price. There's even a pool.

For a key to hotel price categories see p148

General Index

Acknowledgments

Author
Jeffrey Kennedy is a freelance travel writer who divides his time between Italy, Spain and the USA. He is the author of DK's Top 10 Guides to *Andalucía and the Costa del Sol*, *Mallorca*, and *San Francisco*, and co-author of *Top 10 Rome*.

Additional contributor
Stephen Keeling

Publishing Director Georgina Dee

Publisher Vivien Antwi

Design Director Phil Ormerod

Editorial Ankita Awasthi Tröger, Rachel Fox, Maresa Manara, Sally Schafer, Anuroop Sanwalia, Lucy Sienkowska, Jackie Staddon, Hollie Teague, Danielle Watt

Cover Design Richard Czapnik

Design Tessa Bindloss, Stuti Tiwari, Bharti Karakoti, Priyanka Thakur

Commissioned Photography Max Alexander, Peter Wilson

Picture Research Susie Peachey, Ellen Root, Lucy Sienkowska

Cartography Martin Darlison, James Macdonald, Reetu Pandey

DTP Jason Little, George Nimmo

Production Luca Bazzoli

Factchecker Patrick Peterson

Proofreader Susanne Hillen

Indexer Hilary Bird

First edition created by BLUE ISLAND PUBLISHING

Picture Credits
The publisher would like to thank the following for their kind permission to reproduce their photographs:
Key: a-above; b-below/bottom; c-centre; f-far; l-left; r-right; t-top

123RF.com: James Kirkikis 15tl, 10cla.

Alamy Stock Photo: age fotostock / Alvaro Leiva 22-3, / Luis Castañeda 94cla; Ricardo Arnaldo 104-5; Amy Cicconi 63br; Dennis Cox 4cla; Walter Bibikow 43cla,130cb; Enigma 132cca; Jeff Greenberg 77tr, 88b, 97crb; Chris Gug 55tr; Image Source 2tr, 36-7b; JeffG 71b; William S. Kuta 31crb; Maxine Livingston 44tc; Nikreates 108b; NiKreative 41cl; M. Timothy O'Keefe 75tr; Sean Pavone 4b, 4crb; Rosa Betancourt 11tc, 26cr, 34-5, 42t, 53cl, 65cla, 69crb, 73tr, 85tr, 101cla, 124b; Alex Segre 67cl; Stephen Saks Photography 11crb; Paul Thompson Images 62cla; VIEW Pictures Ltd / Dennis Gilbert 25cra; Gregory Wrona 66t; Robert Zehetmayer 3tl, 78-9; ZUMA Press 96tr, 133cla.

The Ancient Spanish Monastery Museum & Gardens: 99tr.

Aventura Mall: Dana Hoff 69tl.

AWL Images: Walter Bibikow 3tr, 138-9; Jane Sweeney 1, 4clb.

Bal Harbour Shops: 102tl.

Balans Restaurants: 86tl.

Big Pink: Gary James 86bc.

Books & Books: 110tl.

Courtesy of Vizcaya Museum and Gardens Archives: Bill Sumner 4cl, 10crb, 20ca, 20br, 21tl, 46t, 106cla, 111b.

Dreamstime.com: Americanspirit 17c, 81t; John Anderson 76tl; Andylid 32-3, 130tl; Sergio Torres Baus 15c; Bennymarty 55b; Tony Bosse 58cl; Darryl Brooks 67tr; Buurserstraat386 47cra; Byvalet 82cl; Brett Critchley 51tl; Songquan Deng 70clb; Tom Dowd 80cla; Dstaerk 4t; Ene 118bc; Russ Ensley 52tl; Fabio Formaggio 24-5; Fotoluminate 2tl, 8-9, 19bl, 52-3; Glen Gaffney 125bc; Giovanni Gagliardi 54cr, 56b; Galinasavina 107br; Alex Grich-enko 40tc; Holocaust Memorial in Miami Beach, Florida, USA / photo Demerzel21 38bc; Wangkun Jia 14bl, 32cla; Stephen Kinosh 122tl; Kmiragaya 6cla, 47bl, 59br, 90cla, 94br; Daniel Korzeniewski 72tl, 92tl; Anna Krasnopeeva 15br; Lavendertime 82b; Marynag 7br, 38t,115tr; Meinzahn 13tl, 14 -5, 17b, 32br, 33cr, 49cl; Meunierd 40b; Dmitry Mitrofanov 99b; Mramos7637 84cla; Sean Pavone 11ca, 16t, 30-1, 30bl; Pitsch22 134cl; Luke Popwell 4cra, 121cra; Yelena Rodriguez 41tr; Romrodinka 50cl; Sborisov 114cla; Siegfried Schnepf 51b; Roman Stetsyk 12-3; Jeff Strand 57crb; TasFoto 31tl, 137b; Tinamou 10cra; Typhoonski 48b, 53tr, Mirko Vitali 25br; Oleksandr Voloshyn 65tr.

Fairchild Tropical Botanic Garden: Jason Lopez 44b.

The Falls: 118cla.

Florida Keys News Bureau: Bob Care 126b; Stephen Frink 54bl; Bob Krist 127cl; Andy Newman 75cl, 129b, 133bll; Rob O'Neal 127tr.

Getty Images: AFP Photo / Jeff Haynes 61tr; Walter Bibikow 116tl; Buyenlarge 116b; Steven Greave 123cla; Jeff Greenberg 18-9; The LIFE Images Collection / Ray Fisher 39tr; LightRocket / Roberto Machado Noa 71tr; Nicholas Pitt 107tl; mural by Serge Toussaint / photo Joe Raedle 98cla; WireImage / Thaddaeus McAdams 64tl, 87crb.

Provided by the Greater Miami Convention & Visitors Bureau www.gmcvb.com: 42bl; Cris Ascunce 18clb,19tl; Bruno Frontino 100cla; Human Pictures 39clb, 115bc.

Inn on Fifth: 136cr.

iStockphoto.com: 6381380 135tl; Pawel Gaul 76-7; irabassi 125tr; Juanmonino 74b; Manakin 16cb, 60tl, 84br; ntzolov 77cl; Rauluminate 73cla; Serenethos 63t; TerryJ 11b.

Jalan Jalan: 102bc.

Joe's Stone Crab: 89cb.

The Kampong: 109cl, Jon Alexiou 56tl.

Kermit's Key West Key Lime Shoppe: 128tr.

The Kravis Center: 60b.

Lincoln Road Mall: 12cl.

Mandolin Aegean Bistro: 103cra.

Miami Dade College: Cristian Lazzari 74cla.

Miami-Dade Parks and Recreation: Fruit & Spice Park 45cl.

Midori Gallery: 112b.

Courtesy of National Park Service, Lewis and Clark National Historic Trail: 35tl.

New World Center: 61cl.

News Cafe: 49tr.

Pérez Art Museum Miami: east façade February 2014, Designed by Herzog & de Meuron, Photo by Armando Colls/Mannyof Miami.com 95t; Daniel Azoulay Photography 43clb.

The Phillip and Patricia Frost Museum of Science: Ra-Haus 59t, 91tr.

Pier House Resort & Spa: One Duval 131b.

Pigeon Key Foundation: 122-3.

Red Fish Grill: Douglas Stevens 119clb.

The Ritz-Carlton Coconut Grove, Miami: 113cr.

Robert Harding Picture Library: Richard Cummins 24bl; Richard Cummins.

SkyBar, Shore Club South Beach: 64b.

South Miami-Dade Cultural Arts Center: Robin Hill 93bl.

SuperStock: age fotostock / Jeff Greenberg 34bl, 48tl, f/ Luis Fidel Ayerves 117cla; Richard Cummins 10cl; LOOK-foto 13br.

University of Miami Lowe Art Museum: 26bc; Myrna and Sheldon Palley Pavilion for Glass and Studio Arts 26cla.

The Wolfsonian - Florida International University: 29crb; Lynton Gardiner 83tl; The Mitchell Wolfson Jr. Collection / Wrestler (1929) by Dudley Vaill Talcott 28bl, / Window grille (1929) Architects: William Harold Lee and Armand Carroll 29tl, / Armchair (1931) by Edwin L. Lutyens 42c, / Radio, Nocturne, model no. 1186 (c. 1935) designer Walter Dorwin Teague 6cra, / Dressing table (1929) designer Kem (Karl Emanuel Marn) Weber 11cra, / Stained glass window, (1930) by Harry Clarke 28cr, / Ceiling and Chandeliers (1925-26) Robert Law Weed architect 28cla.

Courtesy of Wynwood Walls: Martha Cooper 43tr, 72b; Damian Morrow 100-1.

Zoo Miami: Ron Magill 45br.

Cover

Front and spine: **123RF.com:** meinzahn

Back: **Dreamstime.com:** Robert Zehetmayer

Pull Out Map Cover

123RF.com: meinzahn

All other images © Dorling Kindersley. For further information see: www.dkimages.com

As a guide to abbreviations in visitor information blocks: **Adm** = *admission charge.*

Penguin Random House

Printed and bound in China

First edition 2003

Published in Great Britain by
by Dorling Kindersley Limited
80 Strand, London WC2R 0RL

Published in the United States by
DK Publishing, 1450 Broadway, Suite 801,
New York, NY 10018

Copyright © 2003, 2019 Dorling
Kindersley Limited

A Penguin Random House Company

19 20 21 22 10 9 8 7 6 5 4 3 2

Reprinted with revisions 2005, 2007 2009, 2011, 2013, 2015, 2018, 2019

ISSN 1479-344X

ISBN 978-0-2414-1110-0

MIX
Paper from
responsible sources
FSC™ C018179